MW00790945

From the Library of
SHEA POPE

What Others are Saying about *Adoring God*:

"Having sat in Keith's Sunday school classes for two years, I have found his passion and hunger for God contagious and inspiring. Keith's teachings on the character and attributes of God have stirred a longing and desire in me to pursue and intimately know my great and Glorious God . . . to know who God is, not a God of my imagination but the God of Scripture . . . the one true God.

"This new journey to pursue God intimately through the study of His character has given me a higher and bigger view of God. Seeing God in all His glory has changed my whole perspective on reading the Bible and on prayer. My previous views of God, self, sin, and salvation have been drastically confronted and transformed from "me-centered" to more "God-centered" perspectives. I am now free to experience God in a new and fresh way that is not only changing my relationships with God and others, but even with myself.

"Part of my journey in having a higher view of God has been shaped by Keith's teaching about meditating on God's attributes. These times have brought my mind, heart, soul, and will into greater relationship and intimacy with God. They've been times that have also expanded my understanding of who God is and who I am in relation to Him. I am humbled by my affection for our glorious God, and adoring Him is my only response.

"Thank you, Keith, for sharing your passion for God."

— Anna Searcy

"Charles Spurgeon said, 'The highest science, the loftiest speculation, the mightiest philosophy, which can ever engage the attention of a child of God, is the name, the nature, the person, the work, the doings, and the existence of the great God whom he calls Father.'

Keith Knell is a child of God whose attention is engaged in the study of God.

"For as long as I have known him, Keith has been studying God to know Him more intimately and to talk to Him more personally. But Keith is not only passionate to know God and His glory; he longs to walk with others on this journey. I believe if you will join Keith, he will be a reliable companion on the road to greater knowledge of our great and glorious God whom we call Father."

— Scott Patty

"When I first attended one of Keith's small group studies on the attributes of God, I was expecting more of an intellectual connection of God's attributes with biblical facts. However, I soon found God connecting my heart with His.

"At first, I was crushed by the shallow way I had been approaching this most magnificent of persons, the only uncreated being. I quickly recognized I had been foolishly looking upon God as someone like myself—such a tragic error.

"As my inadequate views about God were increasingly replaced with truth, my heart began to swell with love for the only One who is perfect in nature, character, and attributes! It was frightening how far I had strayed from truly knowing the God who has revealed Himself so clearly in the person of His Son, Christ Jesus. It was also truly sobering that I could have gone to my grave and missed the treasures of walking intimately with my Lord as He planned and ordained before creating anything.

"Thanks, Keith, for caring about my soul."

— Tim Searcy

"Over the years, I have found that in every aspect of life, to gain clarity, focus, and identity, I must continually reflect on how I answer the question of, "Who is God?" This single question and my answer to it is the litmus test of why I make the choices I make in every single aspect of my life.

"Out of all the relationships I have ever had in my life, Keith Knell has always been the person who pointed me toward 'Soli Deo Gloria' ('Glory to God alone') in all things. Through friendship, mentorship, and leadership, he has been a constant friend and mentor who continues to challenge me to know, love, pursue, and surrender to our great God in all things."

— Solomon Kafoure

"I've known Keith for ten-plus years and his passion for knowing God shines forth in his life. After being in many Bible studies with Keith, a simple pattern of knowing God has emerged. In order to know a person, you must spend time with him or her, talking, asking questions, listening, and sometimes just being still.

"So we can know God by reading His Word, meditating on His Word, praying, and simply being still and listening. The result of knowing God more deeply is a new understanding and perspective on life and what happens in this world. We see God more clearly. He is elevated to His rightful throne, and we become content being His worshipful possessions—His children."

— Keith McKissock

"When Keith first told me about the format for a Bible study centered on the attributes of God, I must admit my first reaction was to think, 'That's certainly a long time to focus on that!'

"But after the first study, I saw just how foolish my initial reaction was. When we seek to learn about our God through Scripture and prayer, we get something far better than knowledge—we actually start to know Him. At the same time, we see that He is much too wonderful ever to know fully.

"This understanding—that we get to spend our lives getting to know, adore, and worship our Creator and Redeemer—refocused my understanding of everything I thought I knew about the Christian life. Before studying God's attributes, I couldn't see that my views of sin, salvation, prayer, service, and pretty much every part of the gospel were warped by my man-centered, or *me*-centered, view of my relationship with God.

"Taking a closer look at God's character led me to repentance. It also led me to a joy in my salvation that I've never known before."

— Allan Phillips

"About five years ago, I began a study of God's attributes led by Keith Knell. Since then, I have continued to explore this inexhaustible subject through various authors, journaling, personal quiet time, group study, biblical meditations, fellowship, etc.

"Through it all, Keith's passion has been contagious and inspiring. At first, it was more of an intellectual pursuit for me. But it didn't take long for that to change as I pressed into our Great God in hopes of simply knowing Him better and with deeper intimacy.

"The image that comes to mind is a child crawling into his father's lap and quietly staring into his face . . . exploring, adoring, and enjoying . . . being in that relational moment. For me, the goal hasn't been to become a better Christian but to rest in the truths of our great God and enjoy Him!

"Keith has become a wonderful friend and a person in my life who is always eager to discuss the things of God. Whether his personal quiet time has been a mountaintop experience or a valley, he is honest about it and continues to learn from any experience God leads him through. His humble yet persistent pursuit of God has led Keith to a place of sharp and singular focus on this subject. The result of that focus is this book, which I believe will bless anyone who reads it.

"If you want to grow in your understanding of who God is and what it means for you to be His beloved child, this book is for you."

— Charlton Lentz

The sun shall be no more your light by day,

nor for brightness shall the moon

give you light;

but the Lord will be your everlasting light,

and your God will be your glory.

Isaiah 60:19

And the city has no need of sun or moon to shine on it,

for the glory of God gives it light,

and its lamp is the Lamb.

Revelation 21:23

ADORING
GOD

FINDING YOUR
HEART'S DESIRE
IN THE LORD

KEITH KNELL

AVIVA
PUBLISHING
New York

Adoring God
Finding Your Heart's Desire in the Lord

Copyright © 2015 by Keith Knell. All rights reserved.

Published by:
Aviva Publishing
Lake Placid, NY
518-523-1320
www.AvivaPubs.com

All Rights Reserved. No part of this publication may be reproduced, stored in a retrieval system or transmitted in any form by any means, electronic, mechanical, photocopy, recording or otherwise, without the expressed written permission of the author. Address all inquiries to: *www.AdoringGod.com*

ISBN-13: 978-1-943164-21-9

Library of Congress Control Number: 2015908604

Editor: Tyler Tichelaar

Cover & Interior Design: Nicole Gabriel / Angel Dog Productions

Every attempt has been made to source properly all quotes.

All Scripture quotes are from ESV unless specifically stated.

Early Edition, 2015

2 4 6 8 10 12

ACKNOWLEDGMENTS

This book was not created by one person alone. I'd like to acknowledge several people who were indispensable in its creation.

I am thankful to Riese Moelker for being the godly shepherdess over the process of creating this work. Both Thomas Hoffman and Richard Swartz were crucial and gifted writers—creating chapters, outlines, and footnote references. Patrick Snow gave overall guidance to help publish this book. And at just the right time, in God's perfect timing, Shawn Dady provided excellent editing and encouragement.

A sea of friends, family, and coworkers have also provided encouragement over these last several years of teaching, journaling, praying, and discussing the glory of God and intimacy with Him. Out of a vast ocean of relationships, my two close friends, Keith McKissock and Charlton Lentz, have been especially encouraging and supportive, journeying as pilgrims with me.

And to everyone else who has been a key part of my journey (and there are so, so many of you), I simply say thank you. You've all been a blessing from God to me, a blessing amazingly ordained in eternity past and impeccably orchestrated by Him.

Lastly, and most importantly in creating this book, we've all stood on the foundational literary works of some of the great men of Christendom—Stephen Charnock, A.W. Pink, Jonathan Edwards, C.H. Spurgeon—just to name a few.

I hope the reader will clearly see that many, if not most, of the concepts and thoughts in this book are from these great minds, people whom we respect and love, and whom we eagerly wait to meet upon our deaths. I humbly want to give credit where credit is due—to these learned men of the past—and to their shared desire of adoring God.

CONTENTS

INTRODUCTION

Do you have a relationship with God? If your answer is "Yes," I want to ask you another question. Do you *really* have a relationship with God? How well do you know Him? Do you read the Bible to grow closer to God, or are you like many people who, if they read the Bible at all, just read it for its stories or for those nuggets of wisdom they can apply to their own lives? When was the last time you gazed adoringly on Him as you read the Bible?

And when you pray, do you spend most of your time asking God for things rather than seeking to grow closer to Him? In short, are you far more self-centered than God-centered? Be honest with yourself and think about these very important questions. Please don't just breeze past this paragraph without stopping and pondering.

It's all right to admit that you have little to no relationship with God. If that's true, then it's best to admit it and determine whether you would like to change, to grow. Many, perhaps most, people are bored with prayer. They don't feel close to God. If they are honest with themselves, they'll admit they really have an inner urge to ignore God all day long.

Let me say, first off, I understand. Do I have a relationship with God? Yes. Definitely. Is it as wonderful as I'd like it to be? No. Am I growing in my relationship with Him? Yes, by His grace and at His pace. The bottom line is that I have my good days and bad days as I pray and as I meditate on God's Word. As the saying goes, I'm not the man I want to be, but praise God, I'm not the man I used to be.

If you are a Christian, do you spend regular time in private study of God's Word and in prayer? You may call it your quiet time, your devotions, your meditations, or make it part of your daily routine without giving it a name. But the question I have for you is: Do you have a deep and rich time with the LORD? Do you pray for God's nearness to you throughout the day? Do you ask Him to reveal your root sins to you that you might please and love Him by repenting and asking Him to remove that sin from your life? Do you turn from your natural bent of self-centeredness to God-centeredness? If these seem like hard-hitting questions, they are meant to be. I am lovingly challenging you and hoping to excite you as you begin to read a book that could potentially change your life and your relationship with God forever.

I invite you to begin a journey. There is a characteristic cycle to the lives of Christians, and as we spend time in God's Word, meditating, reading, and praying, this cycle becomes more evident and beneficial for spiritual growth and closeness to God. This is the cycle of appreciating God for who He is, realizing how we fail to measure up to who He calls us to be, repenting and seeking His forgiveness, and ultimately, appreciating Him for the grace and mercy He shows us in forgiving our sins.

For example, let's say you are really enjoying God's presence and having great times of meditation and devotion with Him. Then, whether suddenly or slowly, perhaps you are tempted and fall into some sin, or perhaps you simply become aware of a sin that has always been a part of your life and has characterized your thoughts or actions. You might wallow in your self-contempt for a time or let your guilty conscience scare you from spending further time with the Lord. You will likely be feeling guilt, shame, and frustration with yourself and your inability to change. But if, instead, you take all of this to God as you read Scripture, pray, and meditate on Him, you will often be better able to recognize both the guilt and shame you're feeling as well as the root sin involved in your heart. By God's grace, sorrow and repentance for your sin follows, and you gain a deeper understanding of Christ's mediation for your sin. You recognize His forgiveness in that moment. And as you are restored to right relationship with Him, your worship and love for God flow out via the Holy Spirit's work in your heart.

Have you experienced this cycle? If not, perhaps a more God-focused, deeper, and more meditative time spent with Him will cause God to do a new work in you.

Ultimately, my goal in this book is not to teach you how to read and understand the Bible better, but for you to get to know God better, to understand Him more fully and love Him more deeply. Instead of reading the Bible for what you can get out of it, like a life manual or a bumper sticker giving you your inspirational quote for the day, this book will help you to begin to read the Word and ask, "What does this passage reveal about God?" After all, who is the Bible really about? What is its purpose? The Bible is primarily about God unveiling and revealing parts of who He is!

With the goal of knowing God better, one of the main emphases of this book is developing your Christian meditation. Christian meditation is focused on reading Scripture, filling the mind, and musing and reflecting on God. It's often mixed with prayer as well as journaling your thoughts, insights, and observations about who God is and who He is calling you to be. It's a time to be still. Know that God is God. Spend time with Him as He has revealed Himself in the Bible. What you believe about God affects everything in your life. Therefore, meditating on His character is one of the most important things for you to do in your Christian walk. Yet most of us must admit how very little we truly know about God.

In this effort, you might begin to ask yourself questions like: Do I really even desire God, or do I tend to ignore Him? Do I want to change myself in light of who God is? Am I willing to discipline my mind and my heart? Am I open to God's grace through the Holy Spirit? Am I humble, or am I filled with pride and self-centeredness?

Nathaniel Ranew wrote a book centuries ago entitled *Solitude Improved by Divine Meditation*. He recognized that the greatest use of the mind is to meditate on God. But Ranew did not view meditation as a mystical process. Christian meditation is not the repetition of a word or phrase again and again until our minds are emptied. Rather, for him it was a deliberate and focused contemplation of who God is as He is revealed in a portion of His Word and what that reality means for us. As we read and search the Holy Scriptures, Christians are fed by the living and active Word of God. We receive guidance and direction, understand His promises, and so forth. In conjunction with reading, we should also pray and talk with God. And we should meditate by pondering, contemplating, and chewing on the truths of Scripture. The more we do this, the more we will develop a heartfelt fervency in our prayer and reading. In Ranew's words, this kind of meditation is the "grand improver" of both prayer and of Bible reading and studying.

Thus says the LORD, "Let not a wise man boast of his wisdom, and let not the mighty man boast of his might, let not a rich man boast of his riches; but let him who boasts boast of this, that he understands and knows Me, that I am the LORD who exercises lovingkindness, justice and righteousness on earth; for I delight in these things," declares the LORD. (Jeremiah 9:23-24)

Are you still unsure whether you want or need to read this book? Consider the following questions and give honest answers—but not to me or to the person who might have suggested this book to you. Be honest with yourself before God.

When was the last time you spent significant time studying God and His character?

Do you regularly meditate on God's character and ponder who He is?

When you read the Bible, do you read it to learn more about God?

What is it about Christianity that originally attracted you to it as a religion? Does it still attract you? Are there things about Christianity that make you uncomfortable?

Does God Himself attract you, or are you merely interested in the benefits you hope to derive from Him?

As you can tell perhaps by this introductory chapter so far, this book is not intended to be a light read. When done well, this study is weighty and requires both emotional and intellectual efforts. If you will be honest with yourself, you can expect to face weighty truths about God and about yourself. And I urge you to seek increased intimacy and improved relationship with God Himself.

My desire for you as you read this book is to develop and grow a relationship with God, and not just a casual acquaintanceship. I want you to learn how to adore God. I hope God will use this book for you to establish and build a solid relationship with Him. By God's grace, may you learn how to pray and read the Bible well. May you learn deep and rich truths about who God is, and may you also dispel myths in your mind that you may have about Him. And along the way, may you learn more about who you are and what it means to be a child of God in His Kingdom. May you learn both about His glory and also how to glorify Him.

By no means have I written this book by myself. The concepts in the pages to follow stand on the shoulders of theological giants—men like A.W. Pink, Thomas Watson, Stephen Charnock, and Jonathan Edwards, just to name a few. Although many of their original writings can be a challenge to read in today's modern English, I've sought to lift their thoughts from the old parchment and invigorate them with modern language.

And, of course, this book is grounded in God's Holy Word, which I love. God's Word is living and active, and I have referred to it throughout my writing. I have also provided extensive end notes with Scripture references and cross-references to provide you with material for hours of contemplative time pondering the Lord of the universe *in His own words*!

In your pursuit of a relationship with God, may James 4:8, by God's grace, apply to your efforts as you read His Word: "Draw near to God and He will draw near to you."

Are you ready to begin? Are you eager to understand God better and to adore Him, or are you still a bit apprehensive? Perhaps you have a mixture of both emotions. Whatever you are feeling, let's begin and seek God together that we might adore Him more fully!

Soli Deo Gloria!

Preface

HOW TO GAIN THE MOST
FROM THIS BOOK

I hope this book will be one of the most life-enhancing books you've ever read. To that end, I want to provide you with insights into how to get the most out of it.

Each chapter of this book can be separated into three important parts:

1. The body paragraphs
2. The contemplations
3. The footnote references

<u>The Body Paragraphs</u>

The body of each chapter is written about a different attribute of God and a different facet of His character, as you can clearly see from the titles in the Table of Contents. Each chapter provides you with structure to grasp each facet of the glory of God. The paragraphs contain numbered footnote references and should be the starting point to dive into the Scriptures.

The Contemplations

The Contemplations are part of each chapter and are thoughts and observations—contemplations—based on the concepts covered in the chapter itself. These contemplations are in the form of prayers. They are thoughts and ideas based upon the concepts discussed in the chapter and are directed toward God. The contemplations in each chapter provide examples of prayers to the Lord as one meditates, reads the Bible passages, and prays to God in a conversational fashion. They are journal entries that I and others have kept and shared. They contain elements of inspiration, struggles, insights, questions, and much more. They are there to stir your thoughts toward areas you may not have considered as you seek to know God better. Even more, they are an example to follow if you wish to learn to journal, pray, and read differently, not just scanning words on a page, but engaging your mind and interacting *with God Almighty Himself.*

The Footnote References

An abundance of footnote references accompany each chapter. They mostly provide Scripture verses to support the truth of the material discussed in the chapter. They also provide references to other Christian saints and scholars who either contributed to this writing or whom you can read further to go deeper into a concept. Although we are all accustomed to reading books chapter by chapter and ignoring the footnotes, I do not recommend you use this book in that fashion. Instead, the footnotes are by far the most important part of the entire book. You will notice that each footnote has a large number of Scripture references, probably many more than you would have thought at first glance. But I have provided so many so you can meditate on multiple passages, lingering with God in His living and active words of truth. So please, do not just gloss over the footnotes. Follow them and let them lead you to God's Word. Spend time there—meaningful, fruitful time. Enough material is in the footnote references for you to meditate on for hours and days and months and years.

Using All Three Components

Now, let me suggest one way you can use all three parts well.

First, read the entire body of the chapter. Read it all the way through just as you would any book, leaving out the contemplations and the footnotes.

Second, pray to God, asking Him to show you His glory. Ask Him to ignite a passion within you to seek Him. Ask Him to reveal Himself to you as well as to reveal any misconceptions about Him you may hold. Pray that He will help you understand who you are as well—the good, the bad, and the ugly—and help you more vividly see your need for Him. Pray that He will make ever more real and beautiful to you the grace He shows in the gospel. These are just a few areas of prayer to consider prior to diving deeper into the book. Such prayers may make the difference between filling your head with thoughts about God versus actually meeting Him and engaging with Him.

Third, slowly re-read the chapter, stopping at the contemplation point symbols. Read the contemplation that corresponds to the symbol for that section. With pen and paper or journal in hand, perhaps add contemplations of your own, writing down some of your own questions or thoughts that may be similar or different from those provided.

Fourth, read the footnote Scriptures for that section of the chapter. Don't skim or read quickly just to confirm that the passage supports what the chapter has said. Ponder the Scriptures. Pray over them. Pray that the Lord will reveal Himself to you in them. Meditate. Think. Ponder. Take note of your thoughts, insights, convictions, and confessions in your prayer journal. Re-read the Scriptures, the sentences in the chapter, the contemplations, and your own journaling. Repeat the cycle, meander among all the components, pondering further, writing further, praying, journaling, and so on.

As difficult as it may be, do not engage in all these areas in a hurried fashion. Devote time to developing your relationship with God Almighty. Ideally, I envision you spending an hour or so at each session doing this. At such a pace, you will probably cover a chapter per week and finish the book over several months. Furthermore, it is my hope that you will return to the material in this book again and again throughout your Christian life. An ever-deepening relationship with God requires meditation on who He is as He has revealed Himself in His Word. And meditation requires focused, attentive, dedicated time; it cannot be accomplished in a quick and hasty read of this book.

Group Study

You may also choose to use this book as part of a group study. If you do, then I suggest that after spending time in one chapter, you meet each week with your group to share your journal entries, your questions, your struggles, etc. Keep the primary focus of the group discussion on God, and don't let it drift to discussions that ignore God and His character.

Chapter 1

ONLY GOD IS GOD

"The God who made the world and everything in it, being Lord of heaven and earth, does not live in temples made by man, nor is he served by human hands, as though He needed anything, since He Himself gives to all mankind life and breath and everything."

Acts 17:24-25

Let us begin our study of the attributes of God as He began with Moses, when He stated, "I Am." God simply is. This is the doctrine of the *aseity* (uh-see-ih-tee), or "self-existence" of God and how our perfect God has always existed outside of time—from everlasting behind us to everlasting ahead of us. In the unchanging perfection of the "I Am," we will discern how His glory will never increase or decrease. And lastly, we will meditate deeply on what our response should be to His undying love for us.

↑↓1

GOD IS SELF-EXISTENT

One of the first things to consider as we begin to talk about God is the fact that He truly is in a class by Himself. Only God is God. He is the only one in the entire universe about whom this statement is true. Bible scholars long ago termed this the aseity of God. Aseity comes from the Latin word combination of "from" and "self." Aseity has at least three aspects to it: uniqueness, absolute independence, and self-existence.

God is unique. There is only one God—there is nothing else nor anyone else in all existence like Him. Every superlative applies to Him. Only God is the creator of everything, infinitely powerful, and all-knowing. Only God extends His perfect and holy grace to His creation. Only He is supreme. Only He is mighty to save us from our natural sinfulness. Only He is the perfect definition of everything good and pure and worthy of praise.

"Who is like You, O LORD, among the gods? Who is like You, majestic in holiness, awesome in glorious deeds, doing wonders?" [1]

GOD IS COMPLETE WITH OR WITHOUT US

God is also independent of His creation and was complete and content in Himself before creating anything, including humanity. That means He did not create us because He needed us or because He was incomplete without us. In our sinful pride and self-centeredness, we tend to exaggerate our importance and take credit where none is due. If who we are benefits God in any way, He is dependent on us.

1 (Uniqueness of God) Ex 15:11; 1 Sam 2:2; Is 40:18, 25, 44:6, 45:5-6; 1 Tim 6:15-16; Mark 2:7; 1 Kin 8:23; 2 Chr 6:24; Jer 10:6

If what we do benefits God, then we could withhold it and do Him harm. If He needs us, then that would give us influence over God. But Scripture does not support such absurd ideas at all.

> *"For who has known the mind of the Lord? Or who has been His counselor? Or who has given a gift to Him, that he might be repaid?"* [2]

> *"The God who made the world and everything in it, being Lord of heaven and earth, does not live in temples made by man, nor is He served by human hands, as though He needed anything, since He Himself gives to all mankind life and breath and everything."* [3]

> *"If you are righteous, what do you give to Him? Or what does He receive from your hand?"* [4]

So neither our righteousness nor our wickedness changes the essence of God. [5] It can't because He is as whole and complete and blessed as He can be in Himself. Even our obedience is our duty, not a favor we do for God. [6] If we fulfill our duty, it doesn't profit God anything. If we neglect it, it doesn't hurt Him, only us.

---

2 (God is complete) Rom 11:34-35; Job 41:11; Ps 24:1, 50:10-12; Acts 17:24-25; 1 Chr 29:14

3 (All things are from God) Acts 17:24-25; Acts 14:15; Gen 1:1; Ps 33:6, 90:2; Isa 42:5, 43:10-13; Heb 2:10, 11:3; Rev 4:11; 2 Pet 3:5; John 1:3

4 (God is without needs) Job 35:7-8; 1 Chr 29:16; Job 22:2

5 (God is unchanging) Ps 102:26-28; Mal 3:6; Heb 1:11-12, 6:18, 13:8; James 1:17; Num 23:19; 1 Sam 15:29; Rom 11:29; Tit 1:2; 2 Tim 2:13

6 (Our obedience is not a favor) Luke 17:10; John 14:15; 1 John 2:4-5; Eph 2:10; Job 22:2-3, 35:7; Rom 11:35; Deut 32:6; Ps 100:3; 2 John 1:6

↑↓2

GOD HAS ALWAYS EXISTED, BUT TIME HAS NOT

Because God is self-existent, He does not depend on anything because He exists apart from and outside of everything, even time. Time is a created phenomenon. The Bible itself begins with, "*In the beginning, God . . .*" marking the beginning of time as we know it. But the beginning of time was not the beginning of God. He existed at that beginning, and *before* it. "*He is before all things, and in Him all things hold together.*" [7]

If we could read history backwards, before the point where time came to exist, the triune God was there all alone by Himself. He had not yet created heaven, where we tend to think He lives. There were no angels to praise Him. He had not yet created earth or any part of the universe. There was nothing but God—no one but God. [8] That was the state of the universe; not just for a nanosecond, a week, or a thousand years, but forever and ever. In the infinite eternity before time itself was created, this solitary God was self-sufficient, self-contained, and self-satisfied. [9]

> "*Before the mountains were brought forth, or ever You had formed the earth and the world, from everlasting to everlasting You are God.*" [10]

---

7 (God's timelessness) Ps 93:2; Col 1:17; 2 Pet 3:8; Ps 45:6, 90:2, 102:12, 24-27; John 1:1, 8:58; Ex 3:15

8 (God is before time) Ps 102:25-26; Isa 40:28, 57:15; Ps 90:2; Gen 1:1; Heb 1:10; Job 38:4-7; John 1:1-3; Col 1:16-17

9 (God is without beginning or end) Ex 3:14; John 8:58; 1 Tim 1:17; Heb 13:8; Rev 1:8

10 (God is eternal) Ps 90:2, 111:3; Rev 4:8; 1 Pet 3:8

When the triune God existed all alone in timeless eternity past, He was perfectly content and complete. Why? Because He was all He needed in Himself. God is and always has been in a peculiar state of glorious perfection. There is no unmet need inside Him. He was never bored or lonely or restless because He is perfect. Every part of Who He is—His understanding, His love, His energies, and much more—all have their perfect object in Himself.

> *"Stand up and bless the LORD your God from everlasting to everlasting. Blessed be Your glorious name, which is exalted above all blessing and praise."* [11]

GOD'S GLORY NEVER INCREASES OR DECREASES

God is unique, independent, and self-existent. Furthermore, when you add to this His unchangeable nature, it all makes perfect sense. He does not change because in His perfection, to change would be to move from perfection to something less. God's glory, that glory that is part of Who He is at His core and always has been, cannot be increased or decreased. [12] Certainly, He can demonstrate it, He can make it apparent, but perfection cannot be improved upon.

Jesus Christ, God the Son, brings glory to the Father, but what He reveals and demonstrates is the glory that was always there. He doesn't add to the glory He shares with the Father. He humbled Himself, left heaven, was born as a child, healed and taught, suffered and died, then rose from the dead and ascended to glory. However, none of this beautiful and miraculous ministry added in the slightest way to

---

11 (God is unchanging) Mal 3:6; Rom 1:23; Heb 1:11-12, 6:18; James 1:17; Num 23:19; 1 Sam 15:29; Tit 1:2; 2 Tim 2:13

12 (God's glory is unchanging) Neh 9:5; Ps 29:2, 104; John 17:5; Rev 4:3, 22:5; Isa 60:1-2, 19-20; Ezek 1:28; Job 26:14; John 1:14, 2:11; Isa 40:26-29; Luke 9:32; 2 Pet 1:16-17; 1 John 1:1

the glory of God or who He essentially is. [13]

Of course, Scripture does say it is possible for us to honor or dishonor God. It also says that God is "glorified" by His creation for His acts of providence and for His plan of redemption. But these examples have to do with His glory *as it is* presented to us, not as it truly is in His essential being. This glorification has to do with the glory that is *due* to Him, whether or not we recognize it, and whether or not we give it.

If He wanted to, God could have continued alone for all eternity without creating creatures to observe His glory. [14] He did decide to create and to reveal His glory to creation, but that was completely by choice. He did not have to do any of it. He was perfectly content in and by Himself before anything at all was created. And nothing in all of creation, however great or small, adds to His glory even now.

> *"Behold, the nations are like a drop from a bucket, and are accounted as the dust on the scales; behold, he takes up the coastlands like fine dust. Lebanon would not suffice for fuel, nor are its beasts enough for a burnt offering. All the nations are as nothing before Him, they are accounted by Him as less than nothing and emptiness. To whom then will you liken God, or what likeness compare with Him?"* [15]

> *"He who is the blessed and only Sovereign, the King of kings and Lord of Lords, who alone has immortality, who dwells in unapproachable light, whom no one has ever seen or can see.*

---

13 (Glory of the cross) Gal 6:14; 1 Cor 2:2; Phil 2:8-9, 3:3, 7-8; Rom 15:17; John 17:1-2

14 (God's glory) Ps 8, 19:1, 65:5-13; Isa 6:3; Rev 21:23; Ex 3:14; 1 Chr 16:29; Ps 29:2, 89:5-8

15 (God is without needs) Isa 40:15-18; Ps 50:9-12; Mic 6:6-7; Heb 10:5-10

To Him be honor and eternal dominion. Amen." [16]

↑↓3

OUR RIGHT RESPONSE

The only right response to such a God, a unique, independent, self-existent God of unchanging glory, is reverence, worship, and adoration. He is unique and alone in His majesty. [17] Although He is one of a kind, this does not mean that He is to be left alone. He calls us to draw near to Him in worship, to gather with the rest of His people, and then in prayers, singing, public reading, and proclamation of His Word, to be awed by His majesty.

God sustains all things, but He Himself is independent of all things; He gives to all and is enriched by none. This independence, however, does not mean aloofness. It means non-dependence. He doesn't *need* us. But He does love us and calls us to enjoy that love. He wants us to experience it fully, to share it, and to return it.

As we worship Him in His aseity, we should be moved to adoration for the love He has shown, love to which we contribute nothing, but which has cost Him dearly—the life of His only Son, Jesus Christ. [18]

SUMMARY

God is unique in all the universe. In His aseity or "self-existence," He is complete with or without us. He is independent of His crea-

16 (God's kingdom endures) 1 Tim 6:15-16; Dan 2:44-47, 4:34; 1 Tim 1:17
17 (God alone is to be worshipped) Ex 20:4-5, 34:14; Deut 6:13-14; Ps 63:6-8, 69:32, 81:9; Matt 4:9-10; Phil 2:9-11; Rev 4:10-11
18 (Gospel results in worship) John 14:6; Acts 4:12; 1 John 5:20; 2 John 1:9; Heb 10:19-22; Rev 7:9-17

tures. At the beginning of time, He had no need of us, yet He chose to create us and love us utterly—and that is a humbling thought. Our perfect God has always existed outside of time, from everlasting behind us to everlasting ahead of us. In that unchanging perfection, His glory never increases or decreases, no matter what we do. As believers, our right response to such a God is reverence, worship, and adoration.

CONTEMPLATIONS

↑↓1

Lord, what must it be like to have every superlative apply to describe You?

Bring to my mind superlatives that describe You.

How does Your unique ability to save me from my sin make a relationship with You so unique from everyone else? What other thoughts and ideas of You, myself, and others ripple from this fact? Help me to ponder all the facets of this truth.

↑↓2

How can You, God, be complete and content within Yourself? How did You, God, create me?

What sins have I committed as I have exaggerated myself rather than recognizing how absolutely independent You are? How have I sinned by being self-satisfied, self-justified, self-righteous, or self-determining? What other self-hyphenated sins have I committed? Why should I love Your absolute independence over everything? Help me to deepen my appreciation for this truth.

Expose, Lord, areas where I've obeyed You because I was doing You a favor in my mind. Help me recognize more fully that You are complete and blessed within Yourself with and without my obedience to You.

Why should I obey You if it does not benefit Your essence?

↑↓3

As I meditate on Genesis 1:1, help me not to focus on what You created, but rather, let me focus on You prior to creation. I've failed even to recognize that the beginning of Your book, as with the whole book, is really about You and not me and others.

Help me meditate on time, as You have created it.

What is it like never to be bored, restless, or lonely in Your perfection? What does this reveal about me? Please teach me about myself in light of You.

As I reflect on the truth that You never change because You are already perfect, it makes sense not to change. But I've never appreciated that fully; help me ponder our relationship and the differences between us around this truth.

Help me to understand more deeply Your glory. The word glory is important, but it is thrown around so frequently that I fear I don't grasp it well enough. What is Your glory? How do I glorify You? Why should I glorify You? And help me to process the truth that You don't need me to glorify You. I feel I am missing important parts of who You are and who I am. Graciously give me understanding.

Help me to find Bible verses of Jesus Christ glorifying the Father so I may ponder them. Reveal to me where I've been erring in my thinking of Christ in relation to the Father and in relation to me.

Do I really have a solid grasp on revering You, adoring You, worshiping You? Expose areas where I have done this well and areas I have not. Bring Scripture references to my mind to help me meditate upon that I may worship, revere, and adore You in truth and not in error.

Chapter 2

SUPREME AND SOVEREIGN OVER ALL

"Oh, the depth of the riches both of the wisdom and knowledge of God! How unsearchable are His judgments and unfathomable His ways! For who has known the mind of the Lord, or who became His counselor? Or who has first given to Him that it might be paid back to him again? For from Him and through Him and to Him are all things. To Him be the glory forever. Amen."

Romans 11:33-36

GOD'S AUTHORITY IS LIKE NO OTHER

Supremacy and sovereignty are closely related attributes of God. The supremacy of God can be defined as His status of being infinitely greater than any creature—He is the Most High, the Lord of heaven and earth. Sovereignty is the exercise of His supremacy, the doing of what He has authority to do. Because God is supreme and sovereign,

He has the authority and ability to do whatever He pleases. [19] God is "Large and in Charge!"

> *"Yours, O Lord, is the greatness and the power and the glory and the victory and the majesty, for all that is in the heavens and in the earth is Yours. Yours is the kingdom, O Lord, and You are exalted as head above all."* [20]

We gain a better perspective on the supremacy of the true and living God if we consider that the Bible indicates that even though we are the highest creatures of His creation, there is still an infinite distance that separates us from the almighty Creator. If all the inhabitants of heaven and all the citizens of the earth were to join together in revolt against Him, He would not be intimidated. [21] It would have less effect upon His eternal and invulnerable throne than a tiny flea kicking at the foothills of Mt. Everest. The Bible tells us that when the nations of the earth conspire together to defy Almighty God, "He who sits in the heavens laughs." [22]

ALL OF NATURE SUBMITS TO GOD'S SUPREMACY

God is supreme and sovereign over the laws of nature. [23] The Red Sea divided and its waters stood up like walls at His command as He rescued Moses and His people; [24] and the earth opened up as

---

19 (God is supreme and does all He pleases) Ps 47:2, 103:19, 115:3, 135:6; Isa 41:4, 43:13, 46:10; Dan 4:17, 35; Rom 9:19-21
20 (God is over all) 1 Chr 29:11-12; 1 Chr 16:31; 2 Chr 20:6; Rev 5:12-13; 1 Tim 1:17; Ps 115:3, 145:21, 150:6; Isa 6:5
21 (Nothing can stop God) Job 23:13, 42:2; Isa 14:24, 27, 46:10; Prov 19:21, 21:30; Ps 115:3, 135:6; Dan 4:35; Luke 1:37
22 (God is not intimidated) Ps 2:4, 11:4, 37:13, 59:8; Prov 1:26; Job 42:2; Isa 40:22; Jer 32:27
23 (God is sovereign over nature) Job 37:10-13; Jon 1:4, 4:8; Isa 45:7; Amos 3:6; Ps 107:25, 121:6, 148:8
24 (God parted the Red Sea) Ex 14

rebels against His authority fell down alive into the pit. [25] When He gave the order, the sun stood still; [26] and on another occasion the same sun went backward ten degrees on the sundial in the palace of King Ahaz. [27] Iron swam on top of water. [28] Fire did not burn when Shadrach, Meshach, and Abednego were thrown into Nebuchadnezzar's fiery furnace. [29] These things don't happen every day—that is why we call them miracles! But where modern man believes the laws of nature to be inviolable, God has proven Himself to be sovereign over even them.

God is also supreme and sovereign over plants and animals. [30] He made ravens carry food to Elijah. He tamed and shut the mouths of carnivores when Daniel was cast into the lions' den. He commanded a fish to swallow and then to vomit Jonah; and later grew a plant to comfort him and then a worm to attack the plant's comforting shade. [31] This is why the Psalmist says:

> "Whatever the Lord pleases, He does, in heaven and on earth, in the seas and all deeps." [32]

↑↓1

THE HEART OF THE KING IS IN THE HAND OF THE LORD

God is supreme and sovereign not only over nature, but over peo-

---

25 (God opened the earth to swallow rebels) Num 14
26 (God caused the sun to stand still) Josh 10
27 (God controls the position of the sun) Isa 38:8
28 (God caused iron to float) 2 Kin 6:5-6
29 (God controls fire) Dan 3
30 (God is sovereign over plants and animals) Gen 2:19, 6:20; Num 22:28-30; Matt 8:26-27, 10:29; Ps 148:7, 9-10; Luke 5:9
31 (God is supreme and sovereign over ravens, lions, fish, and plants) 1 Kin 17; Dan 6; Jon 1:17, 2:10, 4:6-7
32 (God does all He pleases everywhere) Ps 135:6

ple as well, even in how they think, feel, and act. [33] And it does not matter what position of power someone holds. *"The king's heart is a stream of water in the hand of the Lord; He turns it wherever He will."* [34] God hardened the Egyptian Pharaoh's heart so that he would not listen; [35] He guided the Israelites to the Red Sea. [36] God humbles the proud; feeds multitudes; and makes people go hungry. [37] He protects people from marauding enemies; [38] He permits cities to be laid siege to and be sacked. [39] He is the potter and we are merely the clay in His hands to be molded into useful, beautiful, praiseworthy objects, or to be smashed into pieces as He pleases. [40]

> *"Lord, God of our fathers, are You not God in heaven? You rule over all the kingdoms of the nations. In Your hand are power and might, so that none is able to withstand You."* [41]

OUR SUPREME GOD ORDERS EVERY CIRCUMSTANCE

God supremely orders the various circumstances of everyone's lives according to His own plan and purpose. For example, God

---

33 (God is supreme and sovereign over how people think, feel, and act) Ps 105:24-25, 106:46; Prov 16:1, 9, 20:24; Ezra 6:22; Acts 7:10; Ex 9:12; Rom 11:8
34 (God is supreme and sovereign over kings) Prov 21:1
35 (God is supreme and sovereign over kings) Ezra 6:22, 7:27; Ex 4:21, 9:12, 10:1, 14:4, 17
36 (God led the Israelites to the Red Sea) Ex 13:18
37 (God is supreme and sovereign over people) Deut 8:3, 28:22; 2 Kin 8:1; Hag 1:11; Matt 15:32-38; Ex 1:7, 7:5, 14:4, 18
38 (God protects His people) Ex 34:24; 2 Chron 32:7; Neh 4 and 9; 1 John 5:18; John 17:12; 2 Thess 3:3; Jude 1:24; Eph 3:20
39 (God controls cities) Isa10:5, 23:13; 2 Kin 19:32; Hab 1:6; Ezek 26:7-21; Isa 47:1, 48:14; Jer 5:15
40 (God is the potter we are the clay) Ps 2:9, 110:5-6; Matt 21:44; Dan 2:44; Isa 30:14, 60:12; Jer 19:11; Lam 4:2
41 (God rules over nations) 2 Chr 20:6; Jer 5:22, 10:7; Dan 4:25, 32; Rev 15:4; Ezek 26:7-21; Ps 22:28, 47:8; 1 Chr 16:31

created angels. [42] One of those angels was Satan and other angels joined Satan in rebellion against their sovereign God. As a result, they were expelled from heaven. [43] The rest of the angels remained loyal to God and will for all eternity.

But whichever group of angels we consider, God created them and He chose their status and eventual circumstances. The same was true for Adam and Eve in the garden of Eden. If God had wanted to, He could have made them secure in Eden and unchangeable, like the unfallen angels. But instead, God chose to set them in Eden with the responsibility to obey their Maker under the most favorable conditions known to humanity. [44]

Instead of merely reading the biblical stories superficially, it is helpful to ask the question, "*Why* does God sovereignly do everything that He does?" The short answer is that He does all simply because it is His imperial and righteous pleasure to do so. [45] What right does He have to do what He wants to do? He has every right because He is supreme. He is God and He is sovereign.

Furthermore, God does not do things because He *must* do them a certain way, as if He were under some rule or constraint outside of His supreme and sovereign pleasure. He also does not operate that way because it is the right thing to do. No, the action or inaction of our Lord is the right thing simply and solely because *He* did it. God doing it makes it right. God is, in a real sense, a law unto Himself,

---

42 (God created angels) Gen 2:1; Ps 33:6, 148:2-5; Col 1:16; John 1:3; 1 Cor 8:6
43 (God is supreme and sovereign over angels) 2 Pet 2:4; Jude 1:6-7; Rev 12:7-9
44 (God controls both the good and the bad events) Gen 45:5, 7, 50:20; Rom 8:28; Isa 46:10-11; Job 42:2; Eph 1:11; Ps 33:11; Prov 19:21
45 (God does all He pleases) Ps 115:3, 135:6; Phil 2:13; Dan 4:35; Gen 18:14; Matt 19:26; Job 42:2; Jer 32:17, 27; Mark 14:36; Luke 1:37

so that whatsoever He does is right. [46]

> "Oh, the depth of the riches both of the wisdom and knowledge
> of God! How unsearchable are His judgments and unfathom-
> able His ways! For WHO HAS KNOWN THE MIND OF THE LORD,
> OR WHO BECAME HIS COUNSELOR? Or WHO HAS FIRST GIVEN
> TO HIM THAT IT MIGHT BE PAID BACK TO HIM AGAIN? For
> from Him and through Him and to Him are all things. To Him
> be the glory forever. Amen." [47]

Does it bother you to think that you are not the master of your
own destiny and the captain of your own fate? Are you frustrated
because God does not explain to you every reason for every circumstance in your life? Do you feel that you are entitled to a more
comprehensive answer as to *why* God does what He does? If so,
then maybe you have a misconception about who God is.

↑↓2

MISCONCEPTIONS ABOUT GOD, EVEN AMONG PROFESSING CHRISTIANS

A.W. Pink, in his writings on the supremacy and sovereignty of
God, wrote the following many decades ago:

> The most dishonoring conceptions of the rule and reign of the
> Almighty are now held almost everywhere. To countless thou-
> sands, even professing Christians, the God of Scripture is quite
> unknown.

---

46 (Whatever God does is right) James 1:17; Gen 1:31, 50:20; Ps 119:68; Rom
8:28, 12:2; 1 Tim 4:4; Eccl 3:14; Jer 31:12-14
47 (God is wise) Rom 11:33-36; Col 2:3; Isa 11:2; 1 Cor 1:24, 30, 2:6-7; Luke
11:49; Eph 1:8, 3:10; Ps 139:6

Men imagine the Most High is moved by sentiment, rather than by principle. They suppose His omnipotency is such an idle fiction that Satan can thwart His designs on every side. They think that if He has formed any plan or purpose at all, then it must be like theirs, constantly subject to change. They openly declare that whatever power He possesses must be restricted, lest He invade the citadel of man's free will and reduce him to a machine. They lower the all-efficacious atonement, which redeems everyone for whom it was made, to a mere remedy, which sin-sick souls may use if they feel so disposed. They lessen the strength of the invincible work of the Holy Spirit to an offer of the gospel which sinners may accept or reject as they please.

The god of this century no more resembles the Sovereign of Holy Writ than does the dim flickering of a candle the glory of the midday sun. The god who is talked about in the average pulpit, spoken of in the ordinary Sunday school, mentioned in much of the religious literature of the day, and preached in most of the so-called Bible conferences, is a figment of human imagination, an invention of maudlin sentimentality.

The heathen outside the pale of Christendom form gods of wood and stone, while millions of heathen inside Christendom manufacture a god out of their carnal minds. In reality, they are but atheists, for there is no other possible alternative between an absolutely supreme God, and no God at all. A god whose will is resisted, whose designs are frustrated, whose purpose is checkmated, possesses no title to deity, and far from being a fit object of worship, merits nothing but contempt. [48]

---

48 Pink, A.W. *Attributes of God*. n.p, 1930. Print

God's Supremacy Is A Comfort To His Children

Charles H. Spurgeon, the famous London preacher of the nineteenth century, said:

> There is no attribute more comforting to His children than God's Sovereignty. In the most adverse circumstances, in the most severe trials, they believe that God in His Sovereignty has ordained their afflictions, that He overrules them, and that He will sanctify them all. There is nothing the children ought to contend for more earnestly than the doctrine that their God is Master over all creation—that God is King over all the works He has made—that God rules from His throne and that He has every right to sit upon that throne.
>
> On the other hand, there is no doctrine more hated by the world. There is no truth they have made into more of a football than the awesome, incredible, and absolutely true doctrine of the sovereignty of the infinite Lord. Men will allow God to be everywhere except on His throne. They will allow Him to be in His workshop to create worlds and make stars. They will allow Him to be in His mission to dispense His gifts and blessings. They will allow Him to maintain the earth and secure its foundations, or light the stars at night, or regulate the tides and waves of the constantly-moving ocean.
>
> But when God ascends His throne, His creatures then grind their teeth. And if we proclaim God on His throne, and His right to do as He wills with what is His, to deal with His creatures as He sees fit, without consulting them in the matter; then we are shouted down and insulted, and people turn a deaf ear to us, for God on His throne is not the God

they want or serve. But it is God upon the throne that we love to preach. It is God upon His throne Whom we trust. [49]

↑↓3

MAY WE BEHOLD HIM IN ALL HIS SUPREME GRANDEUR

As you meditate on a supreme and sovereign God, may you behold Him in all His glorious grandeur. May you more deeply understand the truth of Who He is. If you've developed views of Him that are merely figments of your imagination, may He make that apparent to you. God is high and lofty. He is supreme and sovereign. Such is the great God we deal with. He is worthy of our worship. [50]

> *"I blessed the Most High, and praised and honored Him who lives forever, for His dominion is an everlasting dominion, and His kingdom endures from generation to generation; all the inhabitants of the earth are accounted as nothing, and He does according to His will among the host of heaven and among the inhabitants of the earth; and none can stay His hand or say to Him, 'What have You done?'"* [51]

SUMMARY

God is supreme and sovereign over all of creation, and therefore, He has the authority and ability to do whatever He pleases.

Spurgeon, Charles. "Divine Sovereignty." New Park Street Chapel, Southwark. 04 May 1856. Sermon.

50 (God is worthy of worship) Ex 20:2-6; 1 Chron 16:23-31; Ps 29:1-11, 100:1-5, 145:3; Rev 4:8-11, 5:12, 14:7

51 (God is to be praised and honored for His sovereignty) Dan 4:34-35; Ps 96:4, 115:3, 134:1-2, 145:3, 150:6; 2 Sam 22:4; Rev 4:11; 1 Cor 6:19-20

Even the laws of nature will turn themselves inside out and obey Him if He commands it. The heart of the king is in the hand of the Lord and He orders every single circumstance in our lives.

That God is sovereign over all of creation is one of the most basic tenets of the Christian faith. However, it is still possible to have misconceptions about the sovereignty of God, even among professing Christians. Only in the light of the Scripture will any misconceptions we have about God's sovereignty be corrected.

Once we truly understand it, God's sovereignty can actually be a great comfort in times of trouble to His children; because after all, the God who loves us beyond measure, who gave his very Son's life for ours, is in control of everything that happens to us.

And, ultimately, our *acceptance of the glorious justice* of that supremacy brings the best result to our hearts—"the peace that passes all understanding."

CONTEMPLATIONS

↑↓1

You are Lord over all. Over *all*. Lord over the warring nations. Lord over viruses and disease. Lord over poverty. Lord, let this truth wash over me and cause my faith to swell. Help my unbelief!

Sometimes when I see how often Your name is defiled, and just how many people are unified in their rebellion and revolt against You, I tend to forget that You are supreme. Perhaps I'm tempted to despair; I forget that You will be proven right in Your timing, and that *all* will bow before You. Forgive my impatience. Help me to trust in Your perfect plan.

You have dominion over this world and all that is in it, including nature. In countless natural miracles, You have demonstrated Your supremacy. Nothing is impossible for You, not even stopping the earth in this rotation. Not even lifting up the impossibly heavy sea. I marvel, and yet I have little trouble believing that You have that power. I am, however, troubled when You wield that power in a way I can't understand. Like when You use the earth as Your agent to carry out death. My nature wants to ascribe that power to something or someone else, to blind chance or impersonal nature. I *know* You have dominion over life and death, but please forgive me when I question Your choices and Your timing. You are lord over every beating heart. Let me humble myself when I presume to know better than You.

↑↓2

Do I put rules and constraints on Your supremacy? Do I try to bring You lower with my prayers of supplication? Am I trying to talk You into my will rather than bowing low and approaching You in submission to Your will? Lord, please reveal to my selfish agenda when I am too envious, too angry, or too prideful to recognize it.

Wow. It boggles my mind to think that You don't consider what we would think of as "the right thing to do." You considered what You wanted, and did it. And that made it right. Now *that's* supremacy. You are what is "right." I don't have to spend time arguing with myself over whether something You chose to do was right or not. It is a given. It was right because You decreed it. How unsearchable are Your judgments and unfathomable Your ways!

I confess: It does bother me sometimes that I am not the master of my own destiny and captain of my own fate. My soul wages a constant battle to win supremacy over You, while my mind, and sometimes my heart, works to submit. I want to want You to be in charge. Help me to deny those tendencies that seek my own sovereignty. Let my heart yearn a little more every day for You to be master.

Chapter 3

THE WILL OF GOD

"I am God, and there is no one like Me, declaring the end from
the beginning, and from ancient times things which have not been
done, saying, 'My purpose will be established, and I will accomplish
all My good pleasure' . . . . Truly I have spoken; truly I will bring it
to pass. I have planned it, surely I will do it."

Isaiah 46:9-11

GOD'S WILL IS PERSONAL, DETAILED, AND WELL-THOUGHT-OUT

As we find our places in this world, we can ask the question, "What
is God's will for my life?" But as we seek to learn more about who
God is and how we may grow to know Him better, perhaps a more
God-centric question would be "What is the will of God?"

We will get to the particulars of God's will, but first, let us consider
some general truths. Because God is truly a person, He has a mind
and a will all His own. His will is personal. And because He is perfect and powerful, all of His actions are impeccably aligned with

His personal will and effortlessly carried out by Him. What God wills, happens. This cannot be said of anyone else in the universe. Knowing that God personally carries out His perfect will all around us, every part of the day—hour, minute, and nanosecond—should be comforting. Just these few tidbits about God should lead us to hours of pondering, adoration, and worship of so great a person!

↑↓1

God's plan, His communicated will, is also comprehensive and detailed. He has planned humanity, animals, nature—all creation—and also all events that happen to His creation. And when God made His plan, He did not just create a general outline of the future and leave the specifics to fall as they may. It was perfectly planned, each and every detail, so that we might see His glory in the marvelous design. [52]

GOD'S PLAN WAS MADE LONG AGO

The Bible is very clear that God determined everything at once, long ago in eternity past, according to His plan. Everything that has happened, is happening, or will happen is working out as part of His original plan. Unlike us, God does not merely plan ahead for this weekend, or six months, or a thousand years, and then wait and see what happens before He plans the next step. He knows all things from the beginning, before He created even time, because everything is part of God's singular decree as King.

"I am God, and there is no one like Me, declaring the end from the beginning, and from ancient times things which have not

---

[52] (God plans all things) Acts 15:17-18, 2:23; Eph 3:9-11; 1 Pet 1:1-2, 20; Rev 13:8; Rom 8:28; Jer 1:5; 1 Cor 2:9; Prov 16:3-4

been done, saying, 'My purpose will be established, and I will accomplish all My good pleasure'. . . . Truly I have spoken; truly I will bring it to pass. I have planned it, surely I will do it." [53]

Not only is God's plan comprehensive, but it is exclusively His. When God made His plan, He did so freely. Nobody tells God what to do! God was alone when He determined everything—there was no one there to influence His decisions. He was not bound by the laws of nature that we consider absolute. There was not any abstract force pressing against Him or any other external cause that had the slightest influence on Him.

He was totally, completely, and utterly free to decree one thing and not something else. He did not even have to do anything at all! God enjoys the kind of absolute freedom that we can only imagine. And when we think of Him and His plan, we need to remember that God is supreme, independent, and sovereign in every single thing He does or ever has done.

"Who has measured the Spirit of the LORD, or what man shows Him his counsel? Whom did He consult, and who made Him understand? Who taught Him the path of justice, and taught Him knowledge, and showed Him the way of understanding?" [54]

---

53 (God decrees all things) Isa 46:8-11; Ps 2:7; Eph 3:11; Rom 8:28-30; 2 Tim 1:8-9; Acts 2:22-24; Prov 16:9, 19:21; Isa 58:11; John 9:1-3
54 (God freely determined His plan) Isa 40:13-14, 44:28, 46:8-11; Ps 33:11; Prov 19:21; Heb 6:17; Rom 9:11-13; 2 Tim 1:9

↑↓2

GOD DOESN'T NEED A "PLAN B"

God's plan is not just comprehensive and exclusive to Him, but it is sure to come to pass. It is not subject to change and corrections when something new comes up along the way. He does not step in occasionally and re-work it. [55] To an all-knowing, all-wise God, nothing unexpected ever occurs. Nothing ever has or ever will cause Him to go to "Plan B." With us, when we make plans, we do so with limited knowledge and we hopefully grow wiser over time. This is simply not so with God—He is and always has been perfect, all-wise, all-knowing, and glorious.

God's design and process for everything is also absolute and un-conditional. It will be carried out as planned. There are no condi-tions that must be met, or contingencies that must be satisfied, no matter how things might appear from our limited perspective as mere creatures. Whenever and wherever God determined some-thing He intends to happen, He has already, in eternity past, de-creed every means that will bring about that very result.

The same saving God who decreed the salvation of His elect people also decreed that faith would come about in them. [56] This same God says, "My counsel shall stand, and I will accomplish all my purpose." [57] God could not speak with such certainty if His plan depended upon even the slightest condition that might or might not occur. In-

---

55 (God's plan never changes) Mal 3:6; Num 23:19; Ps 33:11, 102:27, 138:8; Heb 1:12, 6:17, 13:8; Isa 41:4; James 1:17
56 (God saves and gives faith) 2 Thess 2:13; Eph 2:8-9; Phil 1:29; Acts 11:18, 13:48, 16:14, 18:27; 2 Tim 2:25-26; Phil 1:29
57 (God is certain about whom He saves) Isa 46:10, 55:11; 2 Tim 2:19; John 10:14, 17:2; 1 Cor 8:3; Phil 2:12-13; James 1:18; 1 John 5:20

deed, God "works all things according to the counsel of His will." [58]

GOD'S PLAN IS WISE

God's plan, being a reflection of Who He is, is also supremely wise. If we believe the Holy Scriptures to be true, then we should know that all He does is with His perfect wisdom.

> *"O Lord, how manifold are Your works! In wisdom have You made them all."* [59]

We should not second guess what God has chosen to do with His universe. [60] We cannot know His purposes and we cannot see the end from the beginning as He can. We should trust in His wise character and know that He has used the best means to accomplish His ends. This wisdom is often, but not always, evident as we see the results of His plan in our lives as well as in history. We only see a very tiny fraction of God's plan, [61] but we should judge from what we do see that the rest is guided by His wisdom.

↑↓ 3

GOD'S PLAN INCLUDED ALL THINGS—YES, EVEN EVIL

Beyond the reality that we are not God and that we do not know

---

58 (God's plan is certain) Eph 1:11; Rom 10:13, 8:28, 11:36; Eph 1:14, 2:10; Prov 16:9; Job 42:2; Ps 138:8; Tit 3:5-7; Philp 4:6-7
59 (God's wisdom) Ps 104:24; Isa 28:29; Ps 139:6, 147:5; Rom 11:33; Prov 3:19; Jer 32:19; Isa 9:6, 40:28; Job 5:9; Col 2:3
60 (God does as He pleases with His creation) Rom 9:21; Job 40-41; Psalm 115:3, 135:6; Isa 14:24, 46:9-11, 64:8; Jer 18:6; Dan 4:35; 1 Chr 29:10-12
61 (God is incomprehensible) Ps 139:6, 145:3, 147:5; 1 Cor 2:10-12; Rom 11:33; Job 11:7-9; Eccl 3:11, 8:17; Eph 3:10; Isa 40:28

His entire plan is a more penetrating question. Since God decreed everything in eternity past, and since evil exists in this world, does that mean that God decreed that evil should exist. The short answer is that God decrees all things, even all sins and all evil. [62]

God ordained in eternity past that evil would exist in this world. This does not, however, mean God is the actual sinner or doer of the sin. "Willing that sin exist in the world is not the same as sinning. God does not commit sin in willing that there be sin. God has established a world in which sin will indeed necessarily come to pass by God's permission, but not by his positive agency." [63]

↑↓4

But Why Evil, Lord?

Regarding evil and sin, the question remains: Why would God decree in eternity past that evil should exist? The short answer is so that all of the glorious attributes of God would be displayed more fully. To expand on this answer, we must first recognize that everything and everyone exists to glorify God. This is the reason for all of creation.

Then, building on that first assumption, think about God's characteristics—love, majesty, justice, holiness, wrath, etc. If sin did not exist in the world, these and other characteristics of God could not be as fully appreciated. If there were no sin, we would also not as fully understand mercy, grace, and salvation or the fear of God's holy anger and wrath. Eighteenth century American preacher Jonathan

---

62 (God decrees all things, including evil) Rev 4:11, 14:7; Prov 16:4, 19:21; Gen 1:1, 50:20; Rom 9:14-24; Isa 55:11; Eph 1:11; Acts 2:23
63 Piper, John. "Is God Less Glorious Because He Ordained That Evil Be?" *Desiring God*. Jonathan Edwards Institute, 01 July 1998. Web. 22 Sept. 2015.

Edwards writes:

> It is necessary, that God's awful majesty, his authority and dreadful greatness, justice, and holiness, should be manifested. But this could not be, unless sin and punishment had been decreed . . . . If it were not right that God should decree and permit and punish sin, there could be no manifestation of God's holiness in hatred of sin, or in showing any preference, in his providence, of godliness before it. There would be no manifestation of God's grace or true goodness, if there was no sin to be pardoned, no misery to be saved from. How much happiness so ever he bestowed, his goodness would not be so much prized and admired . . . . So evil is necessary, in order to the highest happiness of the creature, and the completeness of that communication of God, for which he made the world. [64]

↑↓5

God Is In Control Of All Creation

As one final and probably lighter thought on the subject of God's will, we might ask what life would be like if God had not wisely decreed everything in eternity past. Perhaps like some science fiction movie, the world would be under no control and all that happened in it would be the result of random chance. All prophecy in the Bible would be reduced to mere speculation. God would be reduced in His grandeur, [65] akin to some comic book caped crusader whom one

---

64 Edwards, Jonathan, Edward Parsons, Edward Williams, and Samuel Hopkins. *The Works of President Edwards: In Eight Volumes.* Vol. VIII. London: Printed for James Black and Son, 1817. Print.

65 (God is not diminished) Rom 1:23-25; Jer 2:11; Ps 106:20; Rev 9:20; Acts 17:29; Deut 4:16-18; Isa 40:18-19, 25, 46:5

could only hope would fly in at the right moment and save the day.

↑↓6

Sadly, this is the conscious or unconscious belief of many people to-day, both Christians and non-Christians alike. They are left with less peace, assurance, and comfort than Christians who rely on a high and lofty sovereign who loves them and has worked out a plan for their good and for His glory. [66]

But praise Him, it is not the case that the future is a mystery to God! The absolute truth found in the Bible is that God is in control [67] and rules all by His will and eternal decree. We should be thankful that everything is determined by our God of infinite wisdom and goodness!

↑↓7

Is this a settled conviction in your heart? Does it give you the peace that it should, knowing that all that comes to pass is part of His comprehensive, gracious plan?

> *"Blessed be the God and Father of our Lord Jesus Christ, who has blessed us in Christ with every spiritual blessing in the heavenly places, even as He chose us in Him before the foundation of the world, that we should be holy and blameless before Him. In love He predestined us for adoption as sons through Jesus Christ, according to the purpose of His will, to the praise of His*

---

66 (God's glorious plan for Christians) Rom 8:28-30, 9:24; 1 Cor 7:17, 15:51-52; John 6:39-40; Rev 21:4; Gal 1:15; Eph 4:1, 4; 2 Tim 1:9

67 (God is in control) Gen 18:14; Matt 19:26; Luke 1:37; Jer 32:17; Ps 47:2, 103:19, 115:3, 135:6; Isa 43:13, 46:10

glorious grace, with which He has blessed us in the Beloved. In Him we have redemption through His blood, the forgiveness of our trespasses, according to the riches of His grace, which He lavished upon us, in all wisdom and insight making known to us the mystery of His will, according to His purpose, which He set forth in Christ as a plan for the fullness of time, to unite all things in Him, things in heaven and things on earth. In Him we have obtained an inheritance, having been predestined according to the purpose of Him who works all things according to the counsel of His will, so that we who were the first to hope in Christ might be to the praise of His glory." [68]

↑↓8

SUMMARY

God's will is personal, comprehensive, and well-thought-out. When God made His plan, His communicated will, He did not just create a general outline of the future and leave the specifics to fall as they may. It was perfectly thought-out, each and every detail, so that we might see His glory in the marvelous design. It is also certain to come to pass. It was made long ago, from the deepest of ancient times, and there was never a "Plan B." There was no need. Since He is perfect, His plan was also perfect, start to finish.

God's plan was wise and even included the existence of evil. Why evil? Because without it, the characteristics of God could not be fully appreciated. If there were no sin, we would also not fully understand mercy, grace, and salvation or the fear of God's holy anger and wrath.

---

68 (God's plan for Christians) Eph 1:3-12; Rom 8:29-30; Ps 33:12, 65:4; Col 3:12; 1 Thess 5:9; 1 Pet 2:8-9

A good and sovereign God, in control of our lives, is actually quite comforting to the believer who comprehends it. All that comes to pass is part of His good and perfect plan.

CONTEMPLATIONS

↑↓1

Lord, I cannot fully grasp how You can effortlessly carry out Your will through every part of the day. Your level of control is greater than most people imagine. Help me to process this truth about You that I might live more fully in Your presence and comfort.

Help me see where I struggle with taking control from You. Expose my foolishness where I am thinking I am on the throne of life rather than You.

↑↓2

Since You've ordained everything at once in the past, do You change Your mind? How do I reconcile passages that indicate You relented or changed Your mind with the truth that You planned everything in the past and carry it all out perfectly according to Your good pleasure?

I make plans, change them, grow through them. You have never acted this way. What is that like? What does this reveal about You and how different You are from me?

Why do I change and You do not?

↑↓3

Lord, I would not choose the path You have chosen for me. I don't have Your wisdom. You *are* wisdom. I praise You for being supremely wise and setting the course of history based on that wisdom.

Show areas of my thinking about You that have ignored Your wisdom, complexity, and depth. If I've ignored the harder parts of who You are, then reveal them and teach me more about why I have done so. Help me understand myself better and You better.

↑↓4

Give me faith, Lord, not to second guess what You are doing in the universe, even with the existence of evil. I see only a tiny fraction of Your plan right now; help me judge from what I do see that the rest is guided by Your wisdom.

↑↓5

What kind of God are You that You have ordained that evil exist? As I ponder evil, and how horrific it is, let me see Your goodness and mercy in a new light.

As I ponder evil, give me new insights into You and Your glory and how evil, the existence of something antithetical to You, magnifies Your glory.

↑↓6

I think of how I want absolute freedom at times to create and to plan and to organize. Reveal to me now those things I've created, planned, and organized in the past, and let me ponder their outcomes and how You've fulfilled and not fulfilled those things I wanted.

↑↓7

Lord, when I pray as Jesus did, that "Your will be done," I don't want to say it robotically. I want to mean it wholeheartedly because Your will is good. Help this be a settled conviction in my heart, to recognize that Your will is perfect, loving, and, ultimately, for my own good.

↑↓8

Let me see Your creation today in a new light. Let me see it as Your marvelous creation, designed to show Your glory to me. Please give me new heights of worshiping You. Give me opportunities to bear witness to Your glory as I speak of Your creation to others.

Let me praise You for being the ultimate planner! As I think on the old hymn title, "Whatever My God Ordains Is Right," give me passion for Your overall plan and how You've created it once in eternity past and how You are perfectly orchestrating everything right now and into eternity forever. Wow!

Do I still act as if You step in at key times and then step away and let me do my own thing? Do I think You are sometimes distant, letting me do my thing as I would with a child learning to walk? I think of the "Footprints" poem. Help me to see You carrying me at every point of my life. Reveal words for me to search in Your Holy Scriptures that I might praise Your constant presence.

What will it be like in heaven? What have You ordained for everyone's future? Help me read Your Word afresh with thoughts that You have planned every step.

Give me thoughts of a world not planned by You, with You not in control, and let me juxtapose that against the truth of Your complete plan and control over it all. Let me list the differences that I might praise You as sovereign of everything!

As I meditate on Ephesians 1, let me bask in Your presence. Give me rest and pleasure in You as my holy Sovereign, my all-powerful king.

Chapter 4

GOD KNOWS EVERYTHING

"Such knowledge is too wonderful for me;
it is high, I cannot attain it."

Psalm 139:6

GOD KNOWS EVERY FACT, EVERY DETAIL, EVERY WHISPER

Calling any human a "know-it-all" is not a compliment. But we glorify God when we say that He knows everything. His knowledge is comprehensive.

God knows the past, the present, and the future, and He knows all of it to the minutest, sub-atomic detail. Nothing slips by Him. Nothing happens without Him noticing. Nothing can be hidden from Him. No wonder the Psalmist says, "Such knowledge is too wonderful for me; it is high, I cannot attain it." [69]

---

69 (God has incomprehensible knowledge) Ps 40:5, 71:15, 92:5, 139:6, 17-18; Rom 11:33; Job 26:14, 42:3; Col 2:3; Isa 55:8

In the world around us, He has exhaustive knowledge of every grain of sand, of every stone, plant, animal, bird, fish, and human being on earth. He knows every flower in every field—where they are, which plant dropped the seed from which it grew, and which way it will bob when the wind blows.

As you look up at the stars, consider this. He knows everything about every star, planet, and comet; from when it was created to when it will cease to exist. "He knows what is in the darkness." [70] We marvel at astronomers using their telescopes, astronauts walking on the moon, and rovers and probes landing on planets and comets. But God's knowledge puts these manmade accomplishments in their puny place. As we meditate on our all-knowing God, we understand that His knowledge is jaw-dropping and extraordinary.

↑↓1

God's knowledge is not just vast and comprehensive; it is also perfect. He never gets a fact wrong. He knows the causes and results of everything, and He forgets nothing. He knows everything that happened in all eternity past and all that will happen in our eternal future. He even knows all of the possibilities and contingencies, things that didn't happen but might have.

> *"Great is our Lord, and abundant in power; His understanding is beyond measure."* [71]

---

70 (God's knowledge is perfect) Dan 2:22; Job 12:22, 37:16; Isa 40:26; Ps 139:12; Heb 4:13; 1 John 3:20
71 (God knows all things) Ps 147:5; Isa 40:28; Ps 145:3; Job 37:16; 1 John 3:20; Matt 11:23

God has such an exhaustive knowledge of the past because He determined the past. He made it happen. He knows so much about the present because He is making it happen. And He alone knows precisely what will happen in the future to the last detail because it is He who will cause it to happen. If ever anything at all were to happen without God's direct involvement or His permission, it would have to be independent of Him. And if anything at all were independent of Him, He would no longer be the absolute sovereign ruler of the universe. [72]

On a more intimate and personal level, God is perfectly acquainted with every detail in the life of every being in heaven, on earth, and in hell. [73] "No creature is hidden from his sight, but all are naked and exposed to the eyes of him to whom we must give account." [74] How might an appreciation of the staggering implications of the limitlessness of God's knowledge about us change the way we live our lives? [75]

> *"You know when I sit down and when I rise up; You discern my thoughts from afar. You search out my path and my lying down and are acquainted with all my ways. Even before a word is on my tongue, behold, O LORD, You know it altogether." [76]*

---

72 (God causes all things) Isa 14:24-27, 46:10-11, 45:7; Amos 3:6, 4:13; Acts 4:28; Jer 31:35; Lam 3:38; Mic 1:12

73 (God knows every creature in hell) Job 26:6; 2 Cor 5:10; 2 Pet 2:4; Rev 9:11; Ps 139:8; Prov 15: 3, 11; Acts 10:42; Heb 4:13

74 (God knows all people) Heb 4:13; Prov 5:21, 15:3; Ps 33:13-15; 1 Cor 4:5; Job 14:16, 31:4, 34:21; 2 Chr 16:9; Jer 16:17, 32:19; Zech 4:10

75 (God knows how we live) Jer 11:20, 17:10; Ps 25:4, 37:23, 139:23; 1 Sam 16:7; 1 Chr 28:9; Rom 8:27; Prov 15:11, 17:3

76 (God knows what is in us) Ps 139:2-4; 2 Kin 19:27; John 1:48, 2:24-25, 5:42, 6:61, 64, 16:30; Matt 9:4, 12:25; Ps 94:7

NOTHING IS CONCEALED FROM GOD

It is a very sobering fact that nothing can be concealed from God. "For I know the things that come into your mind." [77] God is invisible to us, but we are not invisible to Him. We are shockingly transparent, vulnerable. We cannot hide in the dark of night or behind closed doors. [78] There is nowhere on earth that we are anonymous to God. The trees of the garden were not enough to hide Adam and Eve. [79] His knowledge is pervasive, all-searching.

No human witness saw Cain murder his brother, but God saw everything. [80] Sarah laughed out loud at the thought of having a baby at ninety years old and felt safe in the privacy of her tent, but the Lord heard her. [81] David went to great lengths to cover up his sins with Bathsheba and Uriah, but before long, the all-seeing God sent one of His servants to say to him, "You are the man!" [82] And to each and every one of us, the Lord says, "Be sure your sin will find you out." [83] In our proud, sinful nature, we want to believe that even God owes us privacy. If we could, we would limit or regulate God's knowledge of who we are and what we do. "The mind that is set on the flesh is hostile to God." [84] We don't want anyone to witness our every act. We don't want anyone to search our hearts or judge our actions. So we try to ignore God.

---

77 (God knows our thoughts) Ezek 11:5, 20:32, 38:10; Ps 94:11; Matt 9:4, 12:25; Rev 2:23; Isa 29:15; 1 Cor 3:20

78 (We can't hide from God) Heb 4:13; Jer 16:17, 23:24; Job 34:21-22; Ps 33:13-15, 139:11-12; Rom 2:16; 2 Chr 16:9

79 (People hide from God because of sin) Gen 3:8-10; Rev 6:15-16; Isa 2:19, 21; Jer 23:23-24; Hos 10:8; Luke 23:30; Ps 139:1-12

80 (Cain killing Abel) Gen 4:8

81 (Sarah laughing) Gen 18:12

82 (David being found out with Bathsheba) 2 Sam 12:1-10

83 (Sin is not hidden from God) Num 32:23; Job 10:14, 20:27; Eccl 12:14; Luke 12:2; Amos 9:2-3; Ps 94:7, 9, 139:7-12; Jer 23:23

84 (People are sinners) Rom 7:18, 8:7; James 4:4; 1 Cor 2:14; Col 1:21; Gen 8:21; Job 14:4, 15:14; Ps 51:5; Rom 5:12

"But they do not consider that I remember all their evil." [85]

Everyone who ignores God and rejects Jesus Christ and His remedy for sin should instead fear God and His absolute knowledge of all our thoughts and actions.

"You have set our iniquities before You, our secret sins in the light of Your presence." [86]

↑↓2

GOD'S OMNISCIENCE IS WONDERFUL

If you are a Christian, the thought of God's omniscience should be a tremendous comfort. When we have reached the end of our own knowledge and understanding and are confused and afraid, we can say, "But he knows the way that I take." [87] When we, in our quiet meditations with God, are pondering our temptations and sins, we should cry out to our all-knowing Lord:

"Search me, O God, and know my heart! Try me and know my thoughts! And see if there be any grievous way in me, and lead me in the way everlasting!" [88]

How we long to be understood and loved! Rest in the fact that God knows you intimately—far better than you can understand

85 Hos 7:2
86 (God is aware of our sin) Ps 90:8; Prov 15:3; Hos 5:3, 7:2; Ps 25:7; Rev 20:12; Hos 5:3, 8:13; Jer 14:10, 16:17; Amos 8:7
87 (People can turn to God) Job 23:10; Ps 139:1-3; 1 Cor 10:13; 2 Pet 2:9; Acts 2:38, 26:18, 20; Luke 24:47; 1 Pet 5:7; Ps 55:22
88 (God knows our ways) Ps 139:23-24; Dan 2:22; Ps 33:13-15, 44:21, 139:1-6; Heb 4:12-13; Job 23:8-10, 34:21; 2 Chr 16:9; Jer 17:10

yourself. "He knows our frame; He remembers that we are dust." [89]

And as we ask Him in our quiet meditations to help us understand ourselves and forgive us of our sins, we also ask Him to lead us not into temptations, and to give us a deeper love for Him. May this glorious cycle of humility culminate in us exclaiming, as Peter did, "Lord, You know everything; You know that I love You (John 21:17)."

↑↓3

KNOWING ALL THINGS IS NOT AN ACCOMPLISHMENT FOR GOD, BUT IS A PART OF HIS NATURE

As we gaze more intently upon the beauty of God, we begin seeing how facets of His character integrate with one another. It is within such intersections of biblical truths that we can better appreciate the impeccable logic of Christianity and worship the God of the Bible. [90]

At the same time, we may feel mentally overwhelmed as we try to understand a gloriously multi-faceted God. [91] When we feel overwhelmed, it's prudent to slow down, be still, and meditate upon God. [92] With Bible in hand, seek God. Open your mind, heart, and soul, and pray to Him to show you His glory by His grace. [93]

---

89 (God knows us better than we do) Ps 103:14; Ps 78:38-39, 139:2-4; Isa 29:16; Matt 10:30; Prov 5:21; Heb 4:12-13

90 (Aseity of God) Deut 4:35, 39, 6:4; 1 Cor 8:5-6; Eph 4:5-6; Mark 12:29; Isa 42:8; Zech 14:9; John 17:3; 1 Thess 1:9

91 (God is incomprehensible, but knowable) Rom 11:33; Ps 139:6; Jer 9:23-24; John 17:3; Heb 8:11; 1 John 2:3, 13; Gal 4:9; Phil 3:10; John 17:3; Col 1:10

92 (Meditate on God's Majesty) Ps 1:1-3, 8:1-9, 19:14, 101:6; Phil 4:8; 2 Tim 2:7; Col 3:1-2; 1 Chr 22:19; 2 Thess 3:5

93 (God shows His glory) Ex 33:12-23; 2 Cor 3:18, 4:6; Ps 4:6; 2 Cor 4:4, 6; 1 Tim 1:11; John 1:14

↑↓4

With a deeper understanding of God's knowledge of everything, and connecting that infinite knowledge with the fact that He decreed everything at once in eternity past, and by His power will bring it to pass, one important facet of "knowing" is worth special attention. This would be God's gracious and intimate love relationship with Christians. He "knows" Christians in a special way. [94]

GOD EVEN KNEW HIS PEOPLE IN ETERNITY PAST

When the word "know" appears in the Bible in connection with God, it describes an intimate affection for the person known. [95] When the word "foreknow" is read in the Bible, it describes a *prior* intimate affection for the person known. God foreknew the people themselves. [96] He foreknew certain people in eternity past.

God chose to love them in a special way in eternity past, not because of anything good in their hearts or their actions, not because of anything that He saw in them at the time or in the future, not because of their choosing Him, but strictly because He decided so. God graciously chose to love intimately certain people. Before the foundation of the world, God singled out certain sinners whom He chose to save. [97] He *knew* them.

---

94 (God knows Christians in a special way) Rom 5:8, 8:37-39; Eph 2:4-5; 1 John 3:1, 4:7-11; Col 2:12-13; 2 Tim 2:11; John 3:16; Rom 8:32; Deut 33:12

95 (God foreknows people) Ex 33:17; Deut 9:24; Jer 1:5; Hos 8:4; Amos 3:2; Matt 7:23; John 10:14; 1 Cor 8:3; 2 Tim 2:19

96 (God foreknows everything) Rom 8:29-30, 11:2; 1 Pet 1:1-2, 20; Eph 1:4-5, 11; Acts 2:23; Rev 13:8

97 (God chooses whom to save) 2 Thess 2:13; Rom 8:29; Eph 1:4; 1 Thess 1:4; 2 Tim 1:9; Rev 13:8, 17:8; Col 3:12

But why does God choose particular people? Simply put, we do not know. We can only say, "Yes, Father, for such was Your gracious will." [98] It was simply His good pleasure to do so. [99] More broadly, why has God chosen certain people to engage in a special love relationship? God's ultimate and overarching purpose is to magnify His own glory, just as that is the purpose of creation and life.

"in order to make known the riches of His glory." [100]

For the Christian who is saved and has been chosen in eternity past for eternal glory in heaven with a glorious God, for those of us He foreknew, our response should be immense humility . . . awe . . . unworthiness. We should also be moved with such gratitude and appreciation of the grace of God that we seek to share the good news, the gospel, with others. [101]

For we know not who is gracefully chosen for eternal glory [102] and who is destined for the eternal wrath of God. [103] Only God knows! And there should be no room for boasting in ourselves, but rather, we should boast in God who is great! We should be moved to more love, more obedience, and a stronger desire to grow in the depth of our relationship with the greatest being in the universe. May God grant us these desires, and may we bear fruit to glorify Him. [104] Amen.

---

98 (Will of God in salvation) Matt 11:24-27; 2 Tim 1:9; Eph 1:5, 9, 11, 3:11; Luke 10:21, 12:32; Gal 1:15; Phil 2:13

99 (God's choice not based on us) Phil 2:13; Rom 3:27, 9:11-13, 16; 2 Tim 1:9; Tit 3:5; Eph 2:4; 1 Pet 1:3

100 (God's choice is glorious) Rom 9:23; Eph 1:6, 11-14, 3:16; 2 Tim 2:10

101 (God's choice is humbling) Rom 3:27; 1 Cor 1:29-31, 4:7; Eph 2:8-10; Judg 7:2; John 3:27; 1 Chr 29:14; James 1:17; 1 Pet 4:10

102 (Chosen for heaven) 2 Tim 2:10; Mark 13:27; Hag 2:23; Matt 24:31; Ps 65:4

103 (God's eternal wrath in hell) Matt 10:28, 13:40, 25:41; Rev 19:20, 20:10; 2 Pet 2:4; John 3:36; Jude 1:7; James 4:12

104 (May we have fruit to glorify God) Ps 96:1-9; 1 Chr 16:23-29; Isa 66:18-19; Ps 22:31, 66:4, 86:9, 96:4-9; Rev 15:4

↑↓5

SUMMARY

God's exhaustive knowledge of all things ought to fill us with holy awe. There is nothing we can do, say, or even think that He does not know about already.

> *"The eyes of the Lord are in every place, keeping watch on the evil and the good." (Proverbs 15:3)*

If we were to meditate on this more often, we might live life much less recklessly, and with less worry. We should realize, as Hagar did, that God is *"Him Who looks after me"* (Genesis 16:13). And we should not only be amazed and humbled by the absolute knowledge of God; we should also be moved to love Him.

He planned our entire lives before we were born. He knows every misstep we've committed and will commit, every indiscretion, every sin, every moral lapse. Even so, not because of these things but *despite* them, He determined to love us. This realization should cause everyone to bow before Him in wonder and worship!

CONTEMPLATIONS

↑↓1

Perhaps I've slipped into thinking that someday I will know all that You know, Lord. If I have had any self-focused sins such as pride in thinking this way, bring them to my mind now that I might see my errors beyond merely a mental misunderstanding. Help me see any sinful disposition if it has been there that I might repent and bask in Your truth only.

71

↑↓2

Make me aware that when I sin, it is *all* exposed to You, O Lord, and with that awareness, help me every day to refrain from depravity, knowing it is You who is watching carefully. Bring this to my mind at all times.

↑↓3

Lord, I have destroyed myself, my nature is defiled. I am saved by Your good pleasure and mercy alone—it is undeserved and astonishing to me. Help me to live in humility, knowing it is You who looks after me, and help me to love You more because of it.

↑↓4

How did You create a star? How do You know its every detail? How do You keep it in its place? Give me grace to meditate on You as I marvel at Your creation and how You create and know all.

↑↓5

I will list the things I am hiding from You that I might see my folly. You know them all, of course. Teach me through this exercise that I might repent and draw into closer fellowship with You. Show me and teach me, my Lord.

You know I feel I have a right to privacy when it comes to those around me. How does that differ from privacy before You? I know it's vastly different, but let me meditate on the differences between men and women versus between us and You.

Chapter 5

GOD ALMIGHTY

"Behold, these are but the outskirts of His ways,
and how small a whisper do we hear of Him!
But the thunder of His power who can understand?"

Job 26:14

Power Belongs To God And To Him Alone

God is almighty. He possesses all power, He is unlimited in His mightiness, and He is boundlessly sufficient in Himself. How awesome is our Almighty!

Seventeenth century English Puritan Divine Stephen Charnock describes God's power this way:

> The power of God is that ability and strength by which He can cause to happen whatever He pleases, whatever His infinite wisdom decides, and His infinitely pure will resolves to do. . . . As holiness is the beauty of all God's attributes, so power gives life

and action to all of them. God's eternal plan would be pointless if He did not have the power to execute them. Without power His mercy would just be feeble pity, His promises an empty sound, His threats a mere paper tiger. God's power is like Him: infinite, eternal, and incomprehensible. It cannot be delayed, restrained, or frustrated by the creature.[105]

↑↓1

"Power belongs to God," and to Him alone. [106] Not a creature in the entire universe has an atom of power except for what God assigns. [107] But God's power does not come from any outside source, or depend on any other authority. It belongs to Him inherently.

Nineteenth century British Baptist preacher Charles Spurgeon describes God's power as follows:

God's power is like Him: self-existent, self-sustained. The mightiest of men cannot add the faintest hint of increased power to the Omnipotent One. His throne does not have or need any bracing. He does not lean on anyone or anything for support. His royal court does not depend on His courtiers, and does not borrow its splendor from His creatures. God is Himself the great central source and origin of all power.

Charnock also describes how power is used as a name of God. [108]

---

105 Charnock, Stephen. *Discourses Upon the Existence and Attributes of God.* Robert Carter and Brothers, 1853.

106 (Power belongs to God alone) Ps 89:13; Ex 15:6; Job 9:4; Rom 1:20; Isa 43:13; Eph 3:7; 2 Cor 6:18; Rev 1:8, 11:17, 16:14, 21:22

107 (Power comes from God alone) John 19:11; Rom 13:1; Acts 2:23; John 3:27, 7:30; Deut 3:24, 32:39; Job 26:14, 40:9; Isa 43:13; Ex 15:6

108 (Power is the name of God) Isa 1:24, 9:6, 10:21, 49:26, 60:16; Gen 49:24; Deut 10:17; Ps 132:2,5; Rev 19:15

In Mark 14:52 we read of 'the Son of man seated at the right hand of Power,' that is, at the right hand of God. God and power are so inseparable that they are treated interchangeably. His essence is vast, and cannot be confined in any one place; it is eternal, and cannot be measured in time; it is likewise almighty, and cannot be limited in regard to action.[109]

↑↓2

GOD IS FAR MORE POWERFUL THAN NATURE WE SEE AROUND US

When we see God's creation around us, such as majestic mountains, lightning, avalanches, and massive waterfalls, we should be in awe of God's power as manifested in it. However, we can mislead ourselves into thinking that God is only just as powerful as those things we are viewing. Yet even God's awesome creation fails to give us a large enough comprehension of His massive and infinite power. God has infinitely more power than what we see demonstrated!

> *"Behold, these are but the outskirts of His ways, and how small a whisper do we hear of Him! But the thunder of His power who can understand?"* [110]

We see just the "outskirts of His ways" in creation, which means even these are only the fringe, the periphery of what He is capable of. In a vision, the biblical prophet Habakkuk saw almighty God scattering the hills and overturning the mountains. As you read the account in the Bible, it is chock-full of vivid imagery of God's power.

---

109 Charnock, Stephen. *Discourses Upon the Existence and Attributes of God.* Robert Carter and Brothers, 1853.

110 (God's power is beyond comprehension) Job 26:14; Hab 3:4; Rev 22:5; 1 Tim 6:16; Isa 60:19-20; Matt 17:2; Job 37:23

Yet we read in Habakkuk 3:4 that the prophet says: "and there he veiled his power." This verse says He is hiding more of His power than He is displaying. The power of God is so inconceivable, so immense, so uncontrollable that the fearful upheavals He causes in nature conceal more than they reveal of His infinite might!

↑↓3

Consider the following passages, taken together: "He trampled the waves of the sea" [111] expresses God's uncontrollable power. "He walks on the vault of heaven" [112] tells of the immensity of His presence. "He walks on the wings of the wind" [113] describes the amazing swiftness of His operations.

This last expression is especially telling. He doesn't "fly" or "run," which would indicate that He was in a hurry, but He walks. And He walks on the "wings of the wind," one of the most unpredictable of the elements, gusting in rage and sweeping along with inconceivable speed. Yet they remain under His feet and He is merely walking, still in complete control!

GOD'S POWER CREATED SOMETHING FROM NOTHING

Let us back up in time to ponder God's power in His act of creation. Before we can work, we must have both tools and materials, but God began with nothing. By His word alone out of nothing, He made all things.

---

111 (God's incomprehensible power) Gen 1:1; Job 9:8; Ps 104:2; Jer 10:12, 51:15; Zech 12:1; Isa 42:5; Acts 17:25; Ex 15:6; Job 9:4

112 (God's immensity) Job 22:14; Col 1:17; Job 12:10; Acts 17:25, 28; Heb 1:3; Eph 4:6; 1 Kin 8:27

113 (God is swift) Ps 104:3; Ps 18:10-11; Isa 19:1; Matt 26:64; Rev 1:7; Heb 4:12

"For He spoke, and it came to be; He commanded, and it stood firm." [114]

Look into the sky on a clear night and consider the millions of shining, twinkling stars. It is a sight of such beauty and wonder that even the committed materialist, who sees only massive spheres of burning gas, is awestruck. A universe filled with suns, some of them hundreds or even thousands of times the size of our own, scattered across billions and billions of miles, presents a spectacle of such magnitude that attributing their existence merely to time and chance not only does not satisfy us emotionally, but it also stretches the limits of credibility. But the truth is even more amazing! All the stars, all the planets, all the worlds, did not come into being by accident. But they did miraculously spring into existence out of nothing. The whole world does not give evidence of being accidental or random, but of being orderly, and planned and finished in exquisite detail. And a mere word of incomprehensible power accomplished all. "Let them be," said God. He did not elaborate; and at once the marvelous elaborate construction sprang into being, decorated with every beauty, displaying innumerable intricate details, and proclaiming among awestruck angels its great Creator's praise. "By the word of the Lord the heavens were made, and by the breath of his mouth all their host (Psalm 33:6).[115]

God's power is also constantly on display in His preservation of creation. [116] No creature has power to preserve itself. [117] Both humans

114 (God created all things) Ps 33:9; Gen 1:1; Heb 1:10, 11:3; Rom 4:17; Rev 4:11, 10:6, 14:7; John 1:3; Job 37:4-7; Ps 33: 6, 148:5-6, 136:5; Isa 42:5; Acts 14:15, 17:24; Gen 1:3; Col 1:16-17
115 Pink, A.W. *Attributes of God.* n.p, 1930. Print.
116 (God preserves His creation) Heb 1:3; Col 1:15-17; Acts 17:27-28; Matt 5:45; 2 Pet 3:7; Ps 66:9
117 (Creation cannot preserve itself) Job 8:11; Matt 10:29; Ps 31:23, 121:3, 7, 127:1

and animals would die if there were not plants for food, and the plants would wither and die if the earth were not refreshed with plentiful rain. So God is appropriately called the "preserver of man and beast." [118]

God is at work throughout the planet, maintaining and preserving creatures of all varieties on both the land and sea. With two-thirds of the planet covered by ocean, the preservation of the earth from the violence of the sea is another instance of God's powerful care. [119] The preservation of the natural world is indeed a long-standing testimony to the power of God.

THE POWER OF GOD CONTROLS SATAN AS WELL AS ALL OF SINFUL MAN

God is also powerfully at work, though invisible to us, in the spiritual realm. Satan is real, and if he were not restrained by God, we would feel his malice much more intensely. [120]

> "The devil prowls around like a roaring lion, seeking someone to devour." [121]

Satan is filled with hatred against God and with fiendish animosity toward men, particularly the saints. If he had his way, he might treat us all the same way he treated Job: sending fire from heaven to destroy our crops and cattle and livelihoods, causing a wind to blow down our houses and kill our children, covering our bodies with boils.

---

118 (God preserves creation) Ps 36:6, 66:9; Heb 1:3; Job 12:10; Psalm 37:28, 41:2, 97:10, 121:4; Isa 27:3

119 (God controls nature) Job 38:11; Matt 8:27; Mark 1:27, 6:51; Ps 65:7, 89:9, 93:4; Luke 5:9

120 (God restrains demonic forces) Mark 1:27; Luke 4:36, 22:31-32; Mal 3:11; Eph 6:11; Ps 3:3, 34:7; Job 1:9-12

121 1 Pet 5:8

But praise God and His power that He keeps Satan on a short leash, preventing him from carrying out greater and more evil actions! Almighty God effortlessly confines Satan to the place and purpose He has already ordained for him!

In a much more visible way, God's power restrains the natural corruption of sinful men. [122] He permits sufficient outbreaks of sin to show what the tragic corruption of human society can carry out. What limitless depravity and selfish evil would prevail in the world if God did not powerfully repress it!

> *"Their mouth is full of curses and bitterness. Their feet are swift to shed blood."* [123]

GOD'S POWER TO EXECUTE JUDGMENT SHOULD FILL US WITH AWE

God is powerful, too, to execute judgment. When He strikes, none can resist Him.

> *"Can your courage endure, or can your hands be strong, in the days that I shall deal with you? I the Lord have spoken, and I will do it."* [124]

Numerous examples exist of God's powerful judgment. [125] In Noah's day, God opened the windows of heaven and broke up the great

---

122 (God restrains the corruption of mankind) Gen 20:6, 31:7; 1 Sam 25:26, 25:34; 2 Thess 2:7; Eph 6:1-4; Prov 13:24, 22:15, 23:13, 29:15
123 (Mankind's depravity) Rom 3:14-15; Ps 109:17-18; Rev 16:6; 2 Thess 2:10-11; John 3:19; Gen 6:5, 8:21; Eccl 9:3; Jer 17:9; 1 Cor 2:14
124 (God's judgment cannot be resisted) Ezek 22:14; Ezek 17:24, 21:7, 24:14; 1 Cor 10:22; Heb 10:31; Eccl 6:10; Isa 33:14; Luke 12:5
125 (Examples of God's judgment) Rev 19:15; Dan 4:37; Gen 18:20-25; Matt 25:31-34; Rom 1:18-32; Isa 63:3

fountains of the deep, and the entire human race (except for those in the ark) was swept away, helpless in the face of His stormy wrath. Sodom and Gomorrah were annihilated in a shower of fire and brimstone from heaven. Pharaoh and all his legions were impotent when God blew upon them and drowned them at the Red Sea. Perhaps most spine-chilling of God's judgments is eternal damnation itself.

> *"What if God, desiring to show His wrath and to make known His power, has endured with much patience vessels of wrath prepared for destruction?"* [126]

God is going to display His mighty power in His judgment upon the wicked, not merely by incarcerating them in hell, but also by supernaturally preserving their bodies as well as souls in the eternal flames of the Lake of Fire. [127] The Almighty can crush us more easily than we can a moth. He can blast us into pieces or cast humans into hell any moment He pleases. [128]

↑↓4

The power of the Almighty should fill us with wonder and allegiance. [129] Christians can most certainly trust in such a God! He is worthy of never-ending, unquestioned confidence. Nothing is too hard for Him. If God were restrained in power and had a limit

---

126 (God's judgment cannot be resisted) Rom 9:22; Jude 1:4; 1 Thess 2:16; Prov 16:4; 1 Pet 2:8; 1 Cor 10:22; Eccl 6:10; Heb 10:31

127 (God's eternal judgment on the unregenerate) Matt 13:40, 42, 50, 3:31-33, 18:8, 25:41; Mark 9:43; Jude 1:7; Rev 20:8-15; John 3:36; Luke 16:24; 2 Thess 1:8

128 (The wicked scoff at God's power) Matt 27:40; 2 Pet 3:3-4; Jude 1:18; Prov 1:22, 3:34, 19:29, 21:24, 29:8; Acts 13:41; Ps 1:1

129 (Praises to His power) Ps 46:10, 56:3-4, 66:4, 68:3-4, 72:18, 111:2, 139:14; Ex 15:1; Deut 31:30, 32:3-4; Isa 61:10; Rev 15:3; Job 37:5

to His strength, we might be discouraged or even despair. But as He is, at His very essence and in every way, the very definition of omnipotence, no prayer is too hard for Him to answer. No need is too great for Him to supply. No passion is too strong for Him to subdue. No temptation is too powerful for Him to deliver from. And no misery too deep for Him to relieve. [130]

> *"The Lord is the stronghold of my life; of whom shall I be afraid?"* [131]

> *"Now to him who is able to do far more abundantly than all that we ask or think, according to the power at work within us, to him be glory in the church and in Christ Jesus throughout all generations, forever and ever. Amen."* [132]

↑↓5

SUMMARY

In this chapter, we studied the power of God and how nothing and no one has power except that God has graciously granted it. We also saw how God's power is infinitely greater than even the most powerful forces of nature around us, and how in nature, His power created something from nothing, and how that same power also keeps Satan on a short leash, always having to ask permission as we see in the book of Job in Scripture. And lastly, we meditat-

---

130 (Prayers and confidence in God as we ponder His power) Ps 11:1, 13:5, 28:7, 31:14, 19, 33:21, 84:11; Isa 12:2; 2 Tim 1:12; Heb 4:15; Josh 1:9; 2 Sam 7:28
131 (God's power is comforting) Ps 27:1; Ps 3:6, 23:4, 3, 56:4, 11, 118:6; Heb 13:6; 2 Cor 12:9; Mal 4:2
132 (God's power is sure) Eph 3:20-21; 2 Cor 9:8; Rom 4:21, 16:25; Jude 1:24; Gen 18:14; Heb 11:19; Job 42:2; Jer 32:17, 27; Matt 19:26; Luke 1:37

ed on how God's power to execute right judgments should give us a deeper awe, reverence, and fear of the Lord God Almighty.

CONTEMPLATIONS

↑↓1

What is it like to be able to do all You desire, having the power to carry out everything You desire? You, Lord, have the power to do anything You please. I, on the other hand, am powerless without Your grace to empower me. You are the "battery" of my entire existence. Let me praise Your power. Teach me how to praise Your power!

↑↓2

Forgive me for feeling at times like I have no need to be empowered by You. I can so easily drift to my selfish, bootstrapping ways and neglect my appreciation of Your power all around me and in my life.

↑↓3

As I read Habakkuk, Chapter 3, give me an awe of You and Your almightiness. Please teach me even beyond a clearer view of You and Your power and help me to discover more about myself as a child of the Almighty.

↑↓ 4

Is there anywhere or anytime that You will display Your power unbridled and in its fullness? In heaven? In hell? No particular Scriptures come to my mind immediately, but help me search Your Word and guide me to understand You better.

↑↓5

It is wonderful to pray to an all-powerful God. Forgive me if I have not thought highly enough of Your power when I pray. I can so easily reduce Your immensity. Display Your power over my list of petitions to help me see the enormity of all You can do with my requests, if You so choose. Help me see even limits that I have placed on You and let them blow away like chaff that You might expand my faith in Your infinite power.

Chapter 6

NEVER CHANGING

"I the Lord do not change."
Malachi 3:6

GOD'S IMMUTABILITY DIFFERENTIATES HIM FROM ALL CREATION

We have lived our entire lives with change. Our experiences, thoughts, and feelings have changed who we are. We can grow in wisdom, but, unfortunately, we can also become more foolish. We have learned things that we once did not know. We have forgotten things we once knew.

Our perspectives and philosophies on life also change over time. Our physical bodies change, growing from the dependency of infancy to the strength and stamina of young adulthood; eventually, they grow weary and we breathe our last faint breath.

Does God change over time like we do? Is God just like us in this way? Absolutely not! God does not change. He is immutable. He has always been exactly as He is now and will be exactly the same in the future. This attribute distinguishes Him from all of His creatures. He is eternally *"the Father of lights with whom there is no variation or shadow due to change."* [133]

All that He is today, He has always been, and will always be. He cannot change for the better, for He is already infinitely perfect. [134] Being perfect, He cannot change for the worse; infinite perfection cannot diminish to finite imperfection.

He has never evolved, grown, changed, or improved. Only He can say, *"I am that I am."* [135] He is entirely uninfluenced by the passage of time, so He does not wrinkle or age. [136] Since each and every attribute of God is perfect, they will always be the same. His glory will never fade. [137]

↑↓1

NOT ONLY IS HIS NATURE UNCHANGING, BUT SO IS HIS MIND
In addition to the character of God, His will never changes; He never changes His mind. God is perfect and His plan for creation is perfect since it proceeded from Him in eternity past. Therefore, He has decreed in eternity past His perfect will that is not subject to change. God does not change His mind from what He perfectly set into place in eternity past. [138]

---

133 (God is unchanging) James 1:17; Ps 102:12, 25-27; Num 23:19; Mal 3:6; 1 Sam 15:29; Rom 11:29; Tit 1:2; Heb 6:18; 2 Tim 2:13

134 (God is infinitely perfect) Ps 18:25-26, 92:15; Mark 10:18; Matt 5:48; Deut 32:4; Job 34:10, 36:23; Gen 18:25; 2 Chr 19:7; Rom 9:14

135 (God is who He is) Ex 3:14; Deut 32:39; John 1:1, 8:58; Heb 13:8; Ps 68:4; Rev 1:4, 8, 17, 21:6, 22:13; Col 1:17; 1 John 1:1

136 (God does not age) Job 36:36; Ps 102:12, 25-27; Deut 32:40; 1 Tim 1:17, 6:16; Rev 4:9, 10:6, 15:7; Dan 4:34

137 (God's glory will never fade) Rev 4:3, 21:22, 22:5; Isa 60:1-2, 19-20; Ezek 1:28, 10:4, 18-19, 43:4-5, 44:4; Gen 9:13-17; Ex 24:16

138 (God does not change His will) Matt 13:35; Matt 25:34; John 17:24; Eph 1:4, 3:9, 11; 2 Tim 2:19; 1 Pet 1:20; Rev 13:8

Some of you while reading this might think of times the Bible references God changing His mind or regretting what He did; [139] however, the Bible is unequivocal in its assertion that God does not change His mind. [140] How do we reconcile these apparent contradictions?

When speaking of Himself, God frequently accommodates His language to our limited understanding. He describes Himself as having physical characteristics and features, like eyes, ears, hands, and so on. He speaks of Himself as "waking," as "rising early," even though He never slumbers nor sleeps. [141]

When God alters His way of dealing with men, He describes this change of conduct as "repenting." But all of these are and always were part of God's original will and design. He has not changed. He does not change. He will not change. And this includes His perfect and glorious will for you and me. [142]

> *"God is not a man, that He should lie; or a son of man, that He should change His mind."* [143]

---

139 (God seems to change His mind) Gen 6:6; Jon 3:4, 10; 1 Sam 15:10-11; 2 Sam 24:16; Ex 32:9-14; Isa 38:1-6; Joel 2:13; Jer 18:8, 26:3, 13

140 (God does not change His mind) 1 Sam 15:29; Ezek 24:14; Tit 1:2; Heb 6:18; 2 Tim 2:13; Num 23:19; Isa 44:28, 46:10-11; Ps 33:11; Prov 19:21

141 (God described in human terms) Ps 44:23, Jer 7:13; Jer 7:25; Ps 73:20, 78:65; Ps 121:4; Isa 40:28, Isa 51:9; Ps 11:4; Heb 4:13

142 (God does not change His will) Ps 33:11, 110:4; Eph 1:4; Tit 1:2-3; Heb 6:17; Rom 11:29; Job 23:13; Matt 25:34; Eph 1:4; Philip 1:6

143 (God is unchanging) Num 23:19; 1 Sam 15:29; Heb 6:18; Mal 3:6; Rom 11:29; James 1:17; Ps 102:12; 2 Tim 2:13; Tit 1:2

↑↓2

GOD IS WORTHY OF WORSHIP—CREATION IS NOT

An infinite difference exists between people and their Creator. [144] We as creatures will always be changeable. Everything and everyone in creation is by nature subject to change. If creation were not changeable, it would be God. For this profound reason, God is worthy of worship and creation is not. It is also a reason for us to show humility before God's greatness.

↑↓3

Living things grow old and die and decompose into their component chemicals. By nature, we tend to become nothing because we came from nothing. Nothing prevents our complete annihilation but the will and sustaining power of God. No one can sustain himself for a single instant.

We are entirely dependent on our Creator for every breath we draw, every beat of our hearts, the firing of every brain synapse. We should be grateful and thank the Lord *"who has kept our soul among the living."* [145]

IF GOD CHANGED, IT WOULD BE DEVASTATING

Consider also how your relationship with God might differ if God were as capricious as your fellow man. We can change our minds on a whim, become swayed by a compelling argument, act fool-

---

144 (People are infinitely different from God) Isa 40:18, 25, 46:5; Acts 17:29; 1 Sam 2:2; Ex 8:10, 15:11; Mic 7:18; Ps 86:8, 89:6
145 (We are dependent on God) Ps 66:9; Ps 31:23, 37:28, 97:10, 121:3-4; Acts 17:28; Heb 1:3; Col 1:17; John 15:5

88

ishly, process truth and wisdom from our self-centeredness, and sometimes become distracted or bored—just to name a few troubling traits of people.

↑↓4

If God were subject to such change, we might pray as if we could argue Him out of what He wants to do. We might pray as if He forgot us or was not aware of our present troubles. We could try to keep on His good side out of fear of His walking away from us. As the famous Puritan, Stephen Charnock, stated so well:

> What comfort would it be to pray to a god that, like the chameleon, changed color every moment? Who would put up a petition to an earthly prince that was so mutable as to grant a petition one day, and deny it another? [146]

As Christians, our gracious Lord will never leave us nor forsake us. [147] And the Scriptures that undergird this love relationship will never change! His unchanging nature, coupled with His other attributes, provides us with peace and ease as we live. His holiness is unchanging—He will always act in a holy fashion. [148]

God's love is unchanging—if He loves you in Christ, then such love will never be withdrawn nor diminish from its infinite depth. [149]

---

146 Charnock, Stephen. *Discourses Upon the Existence and Attributes of God.* Robert Carter and Brothers, 1853.

147 (God will never forsake us) Heb 13:5; 1 Sam 12:22; Ps 37:28, 94:14; Matt 28:20; Isa 41:10; Josh 1:5; 2 Cor 4:9; 1 Kin 6:13, 8:57

148 (God's unchanging holiness) Isa 5:16, 6:3; Ps 99:5; Lev 11:44, 19:2, 20:7; Rev 4:8; Mal 3:6; Heb 6:18

149 (God's unchanging love) 1 John 3:1, 4:8, 16; Rom 5:8; Eph 2:4; Ps 103:17; John 3:16; 2 Cor 2:11; Mal 3:6; Heb 6:18; Rom 11:29

His promises are unchanging—we can therefore rely on them, in faith. [150] The Holy Scriptures' immense reliability as to how God thinks and acts, as well as how we should live, is astonishing when we consider the unchanging nature of our God.

> *"For the mountains may depart and the hills be removed, but my steadfast love shall not depart from you, and my covenant of peace shall not be removed,' says the LORD, who has compassion on you."* [151]

GOD CANNOT CHANGE HIS NATURE TO SATISFY UNREPENTANT SINNERS

Conversely, what is a comfort for the Christian should be terror for others. People who defy God, break His laws, and have no concern for His glory, and still want to go to heaven anyway because they were "good people" grossly misunderstand the Holy Scriptures. They live as though God did not exist; then they expect entrance to heaven because of their good works or passive intentions. But the Scriptures are clear. Jesus is the way, the truth, and the life. God's Word is not subject to change.

His Word is living and active and unchanging. [152] It blesses and it condemns. [153] God has declared, *"Therefore I will act in wrath. My eye will not spare, nor will I have pity. And though they cry in my*

---

150 (Reliability of God's promises) Deut 7:9, 32:4; Heb 6:13-18; Gal 3:14; 2 Chr 6:14; Neh 1:5, 9:32; Dan 7:9, 9:4

151 (God doesn't change His love toward His children) Isa 54:10; Prov 2:8; Ps 97:10, 121:4, 145:20; Ezek 37:26; Heb 6:18; Mal 3:6; Rom 11:29

152 (The Word of God is living and active) Heb 4:12; Isa 40:8, 55:10-11; Luke 21:33; 1 Pet 1:23, 25; Gen 1:3; Mark 4:39

153 (God's law condemns us in our sins) Ex 20:5-6; Gal 3:10-11; James 2:9-11; Rom 3:19-20, 4:15, 5:13, 20, 7:7; 2 Cor 3:9

ears with a loud voice, I will not hear them." [154]

God will not—He cannot—deny or contradict Himself to gratify the lusts and rebellion of those with whom He has no relationship through Jesus Christ. God is holy, unchangingly so. So God hates sin, eternally hates it. [155] This, then, is the cause for eternal punishment of all who die in their sins. [156]

↑↓5

SUMMARY

God is unchanging and steady. He is immutable, which makes Him different from everything else in creation. He cannot change for the better, for He is already infinitely perfect. And being perfect, He cannot change for the worse; infinite perfection cannot diminish to finite imperfection. In addition to the character of God, His will never changes; He never changes His mind. He is worthy of our worship *because* He is unchangeable. If God did change, it would be devastating because it would make Him no better than mankind. We, as believers, rejoice in His immutable nature because it also means His *love* is never changing. No matter what mistakes we make, believers can always trust in God's unfailing and unchanging love toward us. He understands our weakness and loves us just the same. We rest securely in this truth.

---

154 (God's judgment) Ezek 8:18; Ezek 5:11, 7:4, 9, 9:10, 24:14; Jer 21:7; Isa 27:11; 2 Thess 1:8-9

155 (God hates sin) Isa 13:11, 26:21; Rom 1:18-21, 2:5-6; Prov 6:16-19; Acts 17:30-31; Ps 5:4, 5, 10:3; Isa 1:6, 6:3; Lev 20:23; Hos 9:15

156 (Eternal punishment for all who die without Christ's atonement for their sins) Matt 25:31-45; 2 Thess 1:5-10; Jude 7; Rev 14:10, 20:15; Isa 66:15-16; Heb 10:27; 2 Pet 3:7; Mal 4:1

CONTEMPLATIONS

↑↓1

Lord, you are so different from everything and everyone I know and see. All of Your creation is just not You. I praise You and worship You in Your differentness! Bring to mind my foolish ways that I may confess them and rest joyfully in You and the fellowship I have in Jesus Christ's atoning work for such foolishness. Help me to understand how I should walk in less foolishness in the future as I ponder the food of the Scriptures.

What is it like, Lord, never to change? A part of that sounds boring, as I like to change and all I know changes.

Every facet of Your character is perfect and, therefore, not subject to any change. Wow! Let me adore You as I contemplate Your perfection and corresponding unchanging nature. Help me understand a glimpse of such perfection better. I am so imperfect apart from You. Creation groans in its imperfection and fallen state. Is this one way I can understand the grandeur of Your glory better?

↑↓2

You never change Your mind. You've set what I see around me as part of Your plan created in eternity past. Do I, at times, develop complacency at this truth? Do I, at times, act as if You do and can change things along the way, failing to rest fully in Your providence? I'm sure I don't even know the depth of the truth that You don't change Your mind. Teach me, Lord, of myself and my wayward errors about You. Teach me, Lord, greater depths to Your never-changing nature.

What about all those passages that talk about You changing Your mind? Why did You put it in those terms? Why do I get a bit riled up to think that You never change Your mind and that Your words merely "toyed" with those in the Bible as well as with me?

Do You never experience regret? I assume not. What is that like? What would I be like if I never regretted anything I did? It reminds me a bit of myself prior to being saved by Your grace. Hmmm.

↑↓3

Honestly, Your infiniteness wears me out. It's one thing for You to be infinitely loving and gracious in all of Your other characteristics, but are You also infinitely different from me? Maybe a better way to put it is that You are just different than me in every respect. But what about me being made in Your image? Does that mean there are facets of me and of You that are similar? Identical? Even apart from the Holy Spirit? People talk and use the phrase that we are "made in the image of God." Sometimes, they seem to go in some odd directions with that Scripture and perhaps to some aberrant conclusions. Help me to contemplate in Your Word how I am made in Your image.

↑↓4

Do You really never get bored? What is that like? And come to think of it, why do I get bored? What is the nature within me to get bored? Is that a sin? Help me, Father. Teach me.

As I ponder Your promises, such as You "will never leave me," or that Your "steadfast love endures forever," just to name a couple, let me first reflect on who You are and what I am to do with this truth. Second, give me the grace to worship You in prayer. Third, bring to my attention areas I need to confess, such as the fact that I don't always trust those promises. Perhaps worse, I seldom rest in them as I ought. As I repent and also worship You, let me pour out my petitions to You in faith that You keep the promises in Your Word.

I don't appreciate the massive importance of Your Word giving little me the promises You have. Unchanging promises. Unchanging You. Wow! Help me contemplate how these truths affect my prayers to You.

↑↓5

Your Word blesses and condemns. I seldom if ever contemplate how You condemn those who are not Christians. That is so politically incorrect, not to mention just hard for me to stay focused on. Teach me how to read those passages of Your condemnation, wrath, and anger in light of what Jesus Christ has done, and enable me to sit quietly with You, the God of the universe.

Impress upon me the glory of the gospel and the work of Christ on my behalf. Let me praise You afresh as I ponder Your unchanging words of condemnation for sin—condemnation of sin that was paid for by Christ, but not poured out on me, a child of Zion.

Chapter 7

HOLY, HOLY, HOLY

"Who will not fear, O Lord, and glorify
Your name? For You alone are holy."

Revelation 15:4

GOD'S HOLINESS PERMEATES ALL HIS ATTRIBUTES

God is holy. Infinitely and absolutely pure; altogether different and set apart. As we use the term "holy" to describe God, we mean that He is perfectly pure, immaculate and complete in moral character. Nobody but God holds claim to this distinction. When the seraphim before the throne of heaven cry out their praises to the Lord God Almighty, they use the best word they can to describe Him and call out:

"Holy, Holy, Holy, is the Lord of hosts!" [157]

---

[157] (God is holy) Isa 6:3; Rev 15:4, 16:5; Heb 7:26; Ps 16:10, 71:22, 78:41, 89:18; Mark 1:24; Isa 5:24, 60:9; 2 Kin 19:22; Jer 51:5

As we ponder all the facets of God, we should remember that it is His holiness that envelops them all. To paraphrase the Puritan Stephen Charnock:

> God's holiness seems to have a preeminence above all His other perfections and it is the glory of all the rest. His holiness is the beauty of them. All his attributes would be unappealing, lacking luster and honor without holiness to adorn them. Purity is the splendor of every attribute of God.
> His justice is a holy justice, His wisdom a holy wisdom, His arm of power a holy arm, His truth or promise a holy promise. His name, which signifies all His attributes, is holy. [158]

Holiness is foreign to the human mind. We may, for example, mistake holiness with doing good deeds. But since God requires holiness, we very much need to know what holiness truly is. [159] To begin understanding holiness, we must start with God's holiness.

> *"Who will not fear, O Lord, and glorify Your name? For You alone are holy."* [160]

God in His holiness permeates every moral virtue, and He defines every virtue by His holiness. God is absolutely pure without any hint of evil. This means He does not do evil, or even desire anything wicked.

---

158 Charnock, Stephen. *Discourses Upon the Existence and Attributes of God.* Robert Carter and Brothers, 1853.

159 (We have to be told what holiness is) Lev 11:44, 20:25-26; 1 Thess 4:3, 7; 1 Pet 1:15-16; 1 Cor 6:18; 2 Cor 12:21; Eph 5:3; Gal 5:19

160 (God alone is holy) Rev 15:4; 1 Sam 2:2; 2 Sam 22:32; Ex 15:11; Ps 86:8, 89:6; Heb 7:26; Isa 40:25

"God is light, and in Him is no darkness at all." [161]

↑↓1

HOLINESS IS THE DEFINING QUALITY OF GOD'S NATURE

Holiness is the defining quality of God's nature: God is *"majestic in holiness."* [162] The prophet says God has *"purer eyes than to see evil and cannot look at wrong."* [163] His holiness is the very antithesis of our fallen human nature.

By nature, people want things that are unholy. However, God desires that which is holy. God emphasizes His own holiness, purity, and righteousness throughout the Scriptures. Because holiness so unique to Him, it is given special attention in Scripture, as Stephen Charnock observes:

> God is referred to more often as Holy than as Almighty. He is distinguished more by His holiness than by any other trait. The word is used more frequently to describe His name than any other. You never find the phrase "His mighty name" or "His wise name," but "His great name," and most of all, "His holy name." This is the greatest title of honor; revealing the majesty and sacredness of His name. [164]

---

161 (God is righteous) 1 John 1:5; 1 Tim 6:16; Ps 58:11, 77:13, 92:15, 145:17; Job 34:10, 36:23, 37:23; Gen 18:25; Deut 32:4
162 (God is holy) Ex 15:11; Rev 4:8; 1 Pet 1:16; Ps 22:3, 71:22, 99:5; Isa 6:3, 43:15, 57:15; Hab 1:13
163 (God is pure) Hab 1:13; Ps 1:5, 5:4-5, 11:5; 1 John 1:5; James 1:17
164 Charnock, Stephen. *Discourses Upon the Existence and Attributes of God.* Robert Carter and Brothers, 1853.

When the angels cry out their praise to the Lord God Almighty, they don't speak of His power, wisdom, grace, or mercy. The word they use to describe Him is "*holy*," and they call out, "*Holy, holy, holy, is the Lord of hosts.*" [165] Consider carefully what this means to us. Angels witness God in a much different way than we do because they are uncorrupted by sin. It is God's holiness that is celebrated before His throne by these creatures.

God appeals to His own holiness as the standard of truth and faithfulness: "*I will not violate my covenant or alter the word that went forth from my lips. Once for all I have sworn by my holiness.*" [166] God swears by His holiness because it is so much of who He is.

A.W. Pink states that God's holiness "may be said to be a transcendental attribute that, as it were, runs through the rest and casts luster upon them. It is an attribute of attributes." [167] Because God's holiness defines all of His other attributes, "*the beauty of the Lord*," is none other than "*the beauty of holiness.*" [168] God's name is also holy. [169]

At The Beginning, All Things Were Created Holy

Because God is completely holy, we can see God's holiness in all that He does. [170] In the beginning, He pronounced all

---

165 (God is holy) Isa 6:3; Rev 4:8-9, 16:5; 1 Pet 1:16; John 17:11; Ps 99:5; Lev 11:44, 19:2, 20:7, 26, 21:8

166 (God swears by His holy name) Ps 89:35; Amos 4:2; Heb 6:13,17; Gen 22:16, 26:3; Luke 1:73; Ps 105:9; Mic 7:20

167 Pink, A.W. *Attributes of God.* n.p, 1930. Print

168 (Beauty of God's holiness) Ps 27:4; Ps 110:3, KJV; Ps 29:2, 96:9; 1 Chr 16:29; Ex 28:2, 40

169 (God's name is holy) Ps 33:21, 97:12, 99:3, 103:1, 105:3, 111:9; Luke 1:49; Isa 57:15; John 17:11; Lev 22:32

170 (God's work reflects His righteousness, holiness, and justice) Ps 145:17; Deut 32:4; Ps 18:30, 33:4-5; Rev 15:3, 16:7; Hos 14:9

that He made "very good," [171] which He could never have done if there had been anything imperfect or unholy in it. This also includes man, who was made "upright," [172] in the image and likeness of his Creator. All of the angels were created holy. This includes Satan and all of the other angels that fell. We know this because Scripture tells us that they "*did not stay within their own position.*" [173]

God's holiness is also evident in His law. Because the law of God is righteous and holy, all forms of sin are forbidden. Because people have a natural tendency to downplay holiness and righteousness, people often limit this understanding to physical actions. However, Jesus explained that the law did not stop with merely our outward behavior, but also reached into the depths of our heart. [174]

> "*The law is holy, and the commandment holy, and just, and good.*" [175]

> "*The commandment of the Lord is pure, enlightening the eyes. The fear of the Lord is clean, enduring forever: the rules of the Lord are true and righteous altogether.*" [176]

---

171 (God's work is very good) Gen 1:31; Gen 1:4, 10, 12, 18, 25; 1 Tim 4:4; Ps 148:2-5

172 (God made man upright and in His image) Eccl 7:29; Gen 1:26-27, 5:1, 9:6; Eph 4:24; 1 Cor 11:7; James 3:9; Col 3:10; Rom 8:29

173 (God created angels holy) Jude 1:6, 14; Ezek 28:15; Neh 9:6; Ps 148:1-6, 5; Col 1:16-17; Luke 9:26; Mark 8:38; Rev 14:10

174 (Man's heart is sinful) Matt 5:21-22, 27-29; Prov 23:7; Mark 7:21-23; Gen 6:5, 8:21; Eccl 9:3; Jer 17:9; John 3:19; Rom 8:7-8; Tit 1:15

175 (God's commands are holy) Rom 7:12; Ps 119:137; 2 Pet 2:21

176 (God's commands are good) Ps 19:8-9; Rom 7:16; 1 Tim 1:8

↑↓2

God's Holiness Is On Display At The Cross Of Christ

God's holiness is clearly on display at the cross. The atonement displays in a wonderful, yet solemn way God's infinite holiness and just how much He loathes sin. How terrible sin must be for God to punish it by imputing it to His blameless and perfect Son and punishing it through His death on the cross! How holy God is to require such an extreme measure to deal with our sin!

At the cross, we witness the collision of our unholy nature and God's holiness. It is here Jesus Christ mediated and resolved these two conflicting natures. Without the mediation of Christ, God's holiness would run a full uncompromising course over a wicked humanity.

Because God is holy, He hates all sin. He loves the righteousness and justice of the law, and hates everything that contradicts it. His Word clearly says, *"The devious person is an abomination to the Lord,"* and *"The thoughts of the wicked are an abomination to the Lord."* [177] Therefore, God must punish sin.

Every sin that God has ever forgiven has been paid for exclusively by the blood of Jesus Christ. A sinner, saved by God's gracious choice, cannot be forgiven apart from the shed blood of Jesus Christ because *"without the shedding of blood there is no forgiveness of sins."* [178]

We should also note that Scripture tells us that every sin, no

177 (God hates sin) Prov 3:32, 15:26; Prov 6:16-19; Isa 13:11, 59:2; Jer 5:25; Ps 5:4-6, 11:4-7, 15; Lev 20:23; Hos 9:15
178 (Forgiveness of sins requires shedding blood) Heb 9:22; Lev 4:20, 26, 4:14-20, 6:7, 17:11

matter how small we think it may be, is very serious. Scripture describes in detail how a single sin can have serious repercussions extending over long periods of time and people, including the entire breadth of the human population! [179]

HOLINESS IS OFFENSIVE TO SINFUL HUMANITY

This description of God's holiness is foreign to manmade gods found in mythology and false systems of religion. This further evidences the divine inspiration of Scripture. People, by nature, do not really want to believe in God's holiness as described in the Scriptures. Fallen man wants to emphasize personally beneficial attributes ahead of those that do not serve his interests.

People quickly do this with God's holiness because it is such an offensive attribute to sinful humanity. Unbelievers imagine a "god" patterned after their own evil hearts, a god that lets them continue in foolishness and sin. However, God corrects them, saying, "*You thought that I was one like Yourself.*" [180] The holiness of God's character as depicted in Scripture goes against man's natural character and inclination. An incomprehensibly holy God with such a hatred of all sin would never have been conceived by any of Adam's fallen descendants because this would require an admission of their own guilt.

God is too often viewed by some as an indulgent old man who leniently winks at the indiscretions of youth. This is not consistent with the way Scripture describes God. The Scriptures say, "*You hate all evildoers*" and "*God is angry with the wick-*

---

179 (Sin has serious repercussions) Gen 3:1-19; Gen 9:21-25; Num 20:8-12; 2 Kin 5:15-27; Acts 5:1-11; 2 Sam 11-12:1-23
180 (God is not like man) Ps 50:21; Num 23:19; 1 Sam 15:29; Isa 55:8-9; Hos 11:9; 1 Cor 1:25; Job 33:12; Ps 99:2; John 10:29; 1 John 4:7, 5:9

ed every day." [181] Unbelievers refuse to believe in a truly holy God, and by nature protest when His hatred of sin is faithfully brought to their attention. The protests of the unbelievers grow when they are told of the eternal consequences of sin in the Lake of Fire; they are in denial that they are deserving of it!

It is a natural thing for people to hide from God. This is the first demonstrated response people have toward God in Scripture. When God approached Adam and Eve after their first sin, they hid themselves. People by nature do not want anything to do with God's holiness. What a horrifying testimony Scripture gives us of our most basic attitude toward God.

↑↓3

Because God is holy and mankind is sinful, our acceptance on the grounds of good works is impossible. It is impossible for sinful people to produce a good work that would meet the approval of infinite holiness. [182] The best work that sinful man can produce is ruined by sin.

The Bible says a bad tree cannot produce good fruit and that our works are as *"filthy rags."* [183] The apostle Paul asks, *"What partnership has righteousness with lawlessness? Or what fellowship has light with darkness?"* [184] God would have to deny His own holiness and

---

181 (God's perspective on sin) Ps 5:4-6, 7:11; Ps 11:4-7; Nah 1:2, 6; Prov 3:32, 15:26; Isa 13:11; Hos 9:15

182 (Mankind is sinful) Gen 6:5; Eccl 9:3; Rom 8:7-8; Job 14:4; Jer 13:23; John 8:34, 44; Eph 2:1-2; 1 John 5:19; Tit 3:3

183 (Mankind's works are filthy) Isa 64:6; Matt 7:16-18; John 3:19, 7:7; Tit 1:15-16; Isa 59:12-15; Col 1:21; 1 John 3:12; Eccl 7:20

184 (Holiness and wickedness have no fellowship) 2 Cor 6:14; 1 Cor 10:21; James 4:4; Eph 5:6-14; 1 John 1:5-7, 2:11, 15; John 12:35, 15:19; Acts 26:18; Matt 6:24

compromise His own perfection to call any of our works holy and righteous. But what the holiness of God requires, His grace has provided in Christ Jesus our Lord. Every poor sinner who has fled to Him for refuge stands *"blessed in the Beloved."* [185] Praise the Lord for His grace and provision in Jesus Christ!

It is because God is holy that we should approach Him with the highest reverence.

> *"God is greatly to be feared in the council of the holy ones, and awesome above all who are around Him."* [186]

> *"Exalt the Lord our God; worship at His footstool! Holy is He!"* [187]

We are to worship *"at His footstool."* This requires us to take a most lowly posture of humility, flat on our faces before Him. When Moses first approached the burning bush, God said, *"Take your sandals off your feet, for the place on which you are standing is holy ground."* [188] God is to be served *"with fear."* [189] As our hearts are awed by His inexpressible holiness, the more humble our approach to Him will be.

HOLINESS IS REQUIRED FROM ALL BELIEVERS

Because God is holy, we should desire to be conformed to Him. This means to become more and more like Him. He commands us to *"be*

---

185 (God's holiness changes us) Eph 1:6, 12, 4:24; Col 1:13, 3:10; Rom 6:4, 7:6; 2 Cor 5:17; Gal 6:15; Deut 10:16, 30:6

186 (God is exalted for His holiness) Ps 89:7; Ps 47:2, 66:3, 5, 68:35; Rev 15:3-4

187 (God is worshipped for His holiness) Ps 99:5; Ps 132:7; Isa 66:1; 1 Chr 28:2; Deut 7:21

188 (God requires our humility) Ex 3:5; Josh 5:15; Eccl 5:1; Mic 6:8; 1 Pet 3:8; James 4:10; Prov 16:19; Isa 58:5; Zeph 2:3; Luke 14:9-11; Rom 12:3

189 (God is to be served with fear) Ps 2:11, 119:119-120; Philip 2:12; Heb 12:28-29; Prov 1:7; Deut 6:13, 31:12-13; Josh 4:24, 24:14; Ps 34:7-9

holy, for I am holy. [190] We are called to be holy *"in all our conduct."* [191] Holiness is required of each of us, as Charnock explains:

> This is our primary way of honoring God. Our lofty, sentimental notions, our eloquent turns of phrase, our self-important ceremonies on His behalf do not bring Him a fraction of the glory as does our aspiration to have fellowship with Him with unstained spirits, and live *for* Him in living *like* Him. [192]

↑↓4

Living like Jesus Christ is not something we're able to accomplish in our own strength. We must look away from anything that we've substituted for biblical holiness, including whatever goodness we think we may have attained in life. Our attention must be on Christ and His holiness.

As much as He becomes the object of our focus, we become more like Him. Holiness, in the words of Dr. John Snyder, "is living with your heart full of Christ, turning away from the world, and showing these two things by a life that is daily reflecting more of Christ." [193]

In the beginning, people want to hide from God and His holiness. This is the very first hint of our relationship with God as fallen man. But there is wonderful news. God has rescued His people from

190 (Christians are called to be holy) 1 Pet 1:16; Lev 11:44, 19:2, 20:7, 26, 21:8; 1 Thess 4:7
191 (God commands us to be holy) 1 Pet 1:15; 2 Cor 7:1; James 3:13; Matt 5:48; Ex 19:6
192 Charnock, Stephen. *Discourses Upon the Existence and Attributes of God.* Robert Carter and Brothers, 1853.
193 Snyder, John. *Behold Your God.* Tupelo, MS: Media Gratiae, n.d. Print. (Week 6, pg. 117)

the terrible wrath of God against sin. His people no longer hide. In fact, Scripture concludes with the wonderful future reality that God's people will dwell with Him. *"Behold, the tabernacle of God is among men, and He will dwell among them, and they shall be His people, and God Himself will be among them."* [194] This voice is from the throne and announces three times that God Himself will dwell with His people.

Pause for a moment and see how the Bible opens with a sinful mankind hiding from God and His holiness, and concludes with a people who *do not hide from God*. The Scriptures go even further and close with an invitation that stands in stark contrast to the driving out of Adam and Eve at the beginning. Now, instead of being driven away, we are being invited to come near.

> *"The Spirit and the bride say, 'Come.' And let the one who hears say, 'Come.' And let the one who is thirsty come; let the one who wishes take the water of life without cost."* [195]

Since God alone is the origin and continual source of holiness, let us passionately seek holiness that only He can give. Let us respond to the call to dwell with Him.

Let us grow in holiness, without which *"no one will see the Lord."* [196] Let our constant prayer be that He might "sanctify us completely, and may our whole spirit and soul and body be kept blameless at

---

194 (God will dwell among His people) Rev 7:15, 21:3; 2 Cor 6:16; Lev 26:11-12; Ezek 37:27; Heb 11:16; Ex 25:8, 29:45; Zech 2:10
195 (God invites mankind to turn to Him, to come to Him, and repent) Rev 22:17; Rev 21:6; Isa 44:3, 55:1; John 7:37; Matt 5:6, 6:33; 2 Tim 2:22; Luke 5:32, 24:47
196 (Holiness required to dwell with God) Heb 12:14; 2 Cor 7:1; 3 John 1:11; 1 Thess 4:7; Eph 5:5; 1 Pet 2:11; 1 John 3:3; Ps 37:27; Isa 1:16-17

the coming of our Lord Jesus Christ." [197] Amen.

↑↓5

SUMMARY

In this chapter, we focused on the holiness of God and how it is an all-encompassing and pervasive part of His nature. The angels around His throne do not cry out "merciful, gracious, powerful." No. They cry out one word—"holy, holy, holy." Mankind is offended by God's holiness and seeks to downplay it in order to justify doing good works to get into heaven. But God does not tolerate sin in any way, and any good work that man does is tainted by sin. All creation was originally made to be holy until the "Fall" of mankind corrupted it. Christians have fellowship with God, and in doing so, become more like Him and bear fruit, not the least of which is holiness.

CONTEMPLATIONS

↑↓1

Lord, Your Word tells us that the seraphim are in awe of Your holiness. They fall before You in worship and praise.

Your holiness is indeed beautiful! Because of Your holiness, I can trust in Your justice. I can believe Your promises will come to pass. It's Your holiness that allows me to accept the reality of and reason for Your wrath. Lord, bring to my mind now each of Your attributes; let me ponder each of Your characteristics and help me understand how they are made beautiful by Your holiness.

---

197 (God sanctifies us) 1 Thess 5:23; Ex 31:13; John 15:3, 17:17; 2 Thess 2:13; 1 Cor 1:2, 6:11; Rom 6:19-22; 1 John 1:9; Acts 20:32

↑↓2

You have defined Yourself by the word "Holy." You even chose the word "holy" as the name of Your Spirit. Not the "Loving" Spirit, not the "Just" Spirit, not the "Omnipotent" Spirit. The Holy Spirit. And holiness is Your only attribute described in the most superlative form: Holy, Holy, Holy. Holy, holier, holiest. When I call out Your name, let Your holiness be the first thing that comes to my mind, and let me fall down low in response.

I *do* want things that are unholy, don't I, Lord? My sinful nature goes in that direction by default. I find myself longing for the things of this world. I desire that which I should not have. My flesh is in a constant battle with my spirit. Holy Spirit, please grow my affection for Christ and my desire for holiness in such a way that it drives out my unholy longings and pursuits. Help me to be sensitive to what is unholy. Help me to be honest with myself. I am convicted when confronted with how I downplay holiness. Sometimes I do look at the outward expressions of works and consider myself righteous. I forget about my heart. I confess that my heart is wicked while my veneer is righteous. Let my greatest aspiration be holiness! If I love You, I will obey Your commands. I *do* love You, Lord. Increase my love for You. Where am I setting the bar too low in my life? Let me meditate on Your Holy Bible and let it not leave my mouth. Let me be careful to do all that is written in it.

↑↓3

As I truly ponder Your holiness, my response is fear and reverence. You are terrifying, Lord! How can anyone, much less me, even stand in light of Your holiness? How can anyone have a relationship with such a Holy One? And now You gracefully remind me that only could so great a God as You be *so* holy, but You also provide a way for me to stand in Your presence. What an amazing God You are! Praise be to You for choosing a rescue for me, a substitute for me to bear Your wrath.

Jesus, what a price You paid for me! I can't even begin to imagine what it would be like to bear the wrath of God the Father. I consider Daniel's vision and his response to Your presence as someone who was beloved. If that's the fate for those who are loved by You, how could anyone withstand Your wrath? Thank You for saving me from having to know this pain and anguish. Let me now consider the sin of Adam and Eve, Noah and Ham, Moses, Elisha's servant, David and Bathsheba, Ananias and Sapphira. Lord, let me never take for granted how much You despise sin. You despise even my smallest sin. You despise every *single* sin. Don't let me explain away what I perceive to be "small" sins. Convict me and call to my mind everything I do, think, and say that is displeasing to You. Compel me to aim for holiness, and not "pretty good."

↑↓4

Let me think for a moment about Your transcendence. You allow me (through the blood of Jesus) to "boldly approach the throne," and yet Your holiness demands "worshiping at Your footstool." How do those come together? How do I pursue intimacy with such a holy God as You? Give me grace to live in these two realities.

I am in a constant battle not to be conformed to this world. This world offers many trappings, but it is like quicksand—without great care and consideration, I can slowly sink. Please help me to be conformed to You. Sustain me in the discipline and diligence necessary to stay out of the quicksand. Help me always to be on guard and to discern quickly when I'm stuck.

↑↓5

What does my false holiness look like, Lord? With what am I replacing biblical holiness? I want to look more like You, Lord.

Show me how I am hanging on too tightly to this world. Please show me how I am fashioning a "goodness" that allows me to live with one or more feet in this world, and not a holiness that requires a denial of self. Fill me with visions of that which I now only see dimly and only in part. I long for a time where I won't be inclined to hide from You. Lord let me feel an even greater longing for glory. I will get to dwell with You someday! Let *this* be my driving desire; put *this* picture in my line of sight rather than the view of this world. That You are for me and not against me, that You invite me to dwell with You, this is my greatest benefit.

Chapter 8

THE JUSTICE OF GOD

"Great and amazing are Your deeds, O Lord God the Almighty!
Just and true are Your ways, O King of the nations!
Who will not fear, O Lord, and glorify Your name?"

Revelation 15:3-4

God's Justice And God's Mercy Are In Perfect Harmony

Is God's justice at odds with His mercy? "The cross proves that mercy triumphs over justice" is a common assumption, although such an idea is completely false.

All of God's attributes are in perfect harmony. His love is completely compatible with His wrath, which meshes perfectly with His holiness, which complements His sovereignty, which is consistent with His justice. We must be careful not to pick and choose the attributes of God like a smorgasbord and play them against each other so the one we most like is the one that prevails.

Many have so erroneous an idea of the divine clemency that they suppose God is as easy-going as a doting grandparent. They suppose that only in the most extreme and exceptional cases (if indeed then) will He punish the crimes of any with everlasting fire. [198]

But God cannot be so trifled with, and He will be Who He will be.

> *"He loves righteousness and justice; the earth is full of the steadfast love of the Lord."* [199]

Another misconception about justice is the idea that there is a cosmic justice or natural law outside of God that guides Him in His justice. This, too, is unbiblical nonsense. God is totally and completely sovereign and answers to no one and submits to no other authority. He does not submit to any justice, but He determines justice because what He decrees is right. [200]

As the fifteenth century German Protestant reformer Martin Luther said:

> God is a being whose will acknowledges no cause: neither is it for us to prescribe rules to His sovereign pleasure—or call Him to account for what He does. He has neither superior nor equal, and His will is the rule of all things. He did not therefore will such and such things because they were right and He was bound to will them—but they are therefore equitable and right because He wills them. The will of men can indeed be influenced and moved—but God's will never can. To assert the contrary is to un-deify Him. [201]

198 Pink, A.W. "Justice of God." *Studies in Scripture* (1922): n. pag. Print.
199 (God loves justice) Ps 33:5; Ps 99:4, 106:3, 140:12; Lev 19:15; Deut 16:20; Is 1:17, 61:8; Prov 28:5
200 (God rules over justice) Is 9:7; Job 34:12, 37:23; Deut 10:17, 32:4; 2 Chr 19:7; Ps 9:7-8; Rev 20:12-13; Col 3:25; Rom 12:19
201 Luther, Martin, J. I. Packer, and O. R. Johnston. *Martin Luther on the Bond-*

↑↓1

What is the justice of God? It is an essential property in God, whereby He is infinitely just in Himself, of Himself, for, from, and by Himself alone and no other. [202] What is the rule of this justice? His own free will and nothing else—for whatever He wills is just, and because He wills it, it is just, and not because it is just therefore He wills it. [203]

THE DIFFERENCE BETWEEN SOVEREIGNTY, JUSTICE, AND HOLINESS

Since this is the case, some may ask what the practical difference is between God's sovereignty and His justice and His holiness?

Divine holiness has to do more with what God is; Divine justice respects what He does.

"Justice and righteousness are the foundation of His throne." [204]

Sovereignty, too, is part of God's character. He cannot ever *not* be totally and completely in control of everything at all times and in all places. And His justice is how He carries it out.

This brings up a distinction, though, between God's overall, cosmic justice, which He pursues entirely according to His own will and purpose, and justice as He exercises it among His creation. The justice we enjoy is according to His law. [205]

---

age of the Will. A New Translation of De Servo Arbitrio (1525) Martin Luther's Reply to Erasmus of Rotterdam. Westwood, NJ: Revell, 1957. Print.

202 (God is just) Job 8:3, 34:12; Prov 11:1; 2 Chr 19:7; Is 30:18, 61:8; Deut 32:4; Ps 9:7-8, 140:12; Deut 10:18

203 Pink, A.W. "Justice of God." *Studies in Scripture* (1922): n. pag. Print.

204 (God is both just and righteous) Psalm 97:2

205 (God's law is just) Col 3:25; Ps 19:7-8, 111:7, 119:142; Rom 7:7, 12

Nothing compelled Him to issue a law, and nothing constrained Him as to what that law might contain. But once He created a moral universe in which His justice would prevail and once He revealed His will and His law to humanity, He became the supreme governor of human justice. This is the justice we are more familiar with in which the dictates of the law are carried out fairly for everyone. As Thomas Merton, Catholic author, discussed God's justice:

> God is absolute Lord and also governor and judge of the world. [206] As absolute Lord, His justice is nothing but the absolute and free exercise of His own will concerning His creatures. In this respect, God . . . has no other rule but His own will: He does not will things because they are just—but, therefore, they are just because He wills them. He has a right to make and frame anything as He wills in any manner that pleases Him . . . As governor and judge, He gives a law to His creatures and His governing justice consists in giving all their due according to His law. [207]

↑↓2

GOD'S JUSTICE SHOULD BE OUR PASSION

Christians are to reflect His character in every way. This means that justice should be our passion, too, because it reflects both His character and His stated will. The first patriarch, Abraham, consoled himself with the fact that:

"The judge of all the earth" would assuredly *"do right."* [208]

---

206 (God is the judge of the world) Ps 9:7-8; Rev 20:12-13; Is 66:24; Col 3:25; Gen 18:25; Rom 2:16, 3:5-6; Eccl 12:14
207 Pink, A.W. "Justice of God." *Studies in Scripture* (1922): n. pag. Print.
208 (God's law is just) Gen. 18:25; Deut 10:18, 31:26, 32:4; Ps 140:12

Moses declared:

"I will proclaim the name of the Lord. Oh, praise the greatness of our God! He is the Rock, His works are perfect, and all His ways are just. A faithful God who does no wrong, upright and just is He." [209]

God's justice was a recurring theme in the Psalms and wisdom literature and New Testament teaching on Kingdom living.

"To do righteousness and justice is more acceptable to the Lord than sacrifice." [210]

David was the prime example of executing God's justice among His people. He is always considered the greatest monarch of Israel but not because of his military exploits or even the purity of worship he practiced and encouraged.

"David reigned over all Israel. And David administered justice and equity to all His people." [211]

And his son, Solomon, was known for wisdom and riches, but even the Queen of Sheba recognized his greatest achievement was ruling with justice.

"Blessed be the Lord your God, who has delighted in you and set you on the throne of Israel! Because the Lord loved Israel forever, He has made you king, that you may execute justice and righteousness." [212]

---

209 (God's law is perfect) Deut 32:3, 4; Dan 4:37; Matt 5:48; Rev 15:3; Ps 19:7-9, 119:137; 2 Pet 2:21; Rom 7:12,16
210 (Christians should be just) Prov 11:1, 18:5, 21:3, 21:15; Ps 11:7, 33:5, 112:5, 119:4; Phil 4:8
211 (David was a just king) 2 Sam 8:15
212 (Solomon was a just king) 1 Kin 10:9

And we, too, should seek to promote justice in our various spheres of our influence. None of us is a king, but there is always room for inequality and wickedness and, therefore, a need for justice in our homes, workplaces, and even our churches. [213]

↑↓3

GOD WILL ULTIMATELY CORRECT INJUSTICE

God has promised to govern His creation justly, and so we know it will happen. But injustice is all around us. It grieves us and makes us impatient for God to act—to dispense justice and make things right. When injustice continues, we may begin to wonder whether He sees, or cares, or intends to do anything after all.

> We all growl like bears; we moan and moan like doves; we hope for justice, but there is none; for salvation, but it is far from us. Justice is turned back, and righteousness stands far away; for truth has stumbled in the public squares, and uprightness cannot enter. Truth is lacking, and he who departs from evil makes himself a prey. [214]

Or in the words of St. Augustine, "Where is the reward of my good life? Where is the wage of my service? I live well and am in need; and the unjust man abounds." [215]

It does seem sometimes that injustice prevails and God does nothing. It has been the experience of patriarchs, the lament of proph-

---

213 (Christians should be just) 1 Cor 11:17-22; James 2:1; Prov 11:1, 18:5, 21:15; Philip 4:8
214 (We yearn for God's justice) Is 59:11, 14-15; Rev 6:10; Is 30:18; Luke 11:32; Rev 11:18; John 16:8
215 Augustine, St. *Expositions on the Psalms.* N.p.: n.p., n.d.

ets and Psalmists, and the cry of martyred saints. [216]

But still, God is just and good and sovereign. He is still aware of the injustices His people suffer—more aware than we are. And He will act at the proper time. We must never take His delay as a miscarriage of justice.

> *"Fret not yourself because of the evildoers; fret not yourself over the one who prospers in His way, over the man who carries out evil devices!"* [217]

God, in His inscrutable timing, will right every wrong, will correct every injustice, and punish every crime. Ultimate justice will come at the hands of Christ, the one true and just governor.

> *"A throne will be established in steadfast love, and on it will sit in faithfulness in the tent of David one who judges and seeks justice and is swift to do righteousness."* [218]

We must trust in God's timing for the ultimate execution of His justice. The alternatives are despair or revenge; we either give up on the idea of justice altogether, or we take matters into our own hands. Neither one is appropriate.

> *"You have wearied the Lord with your words. . . . by asking, 'Where is the God of justice?'"* [219]

---

216 (We yearn for God's justice) Gen 40:23; Job 12:6, 21:7; Jer 12:1; Ps 10:12-15, 35:17-22; Rev 6:10

217 (God will make all right) Ps 37:1-7; Prov 24:19; Is 30:18; Matt 3:7; Luke 3:7; 1 Thess 1:10; Rev 14:7, 20:11-13; 1 Pet 4:5; Eccl 12:14

218 (Christ will bring ultimate justice) Is 16:5; 2 Thess 1:8-9; Jer 23:5; Acts 17:31, 24:25; John 5:22, 9:39; Rom 2:16; 2 Tim 4:1; Rev 19:11

219 (Christians can trust God's timing for justice) Mal 2:17; Deut 32:35; Rom 12:19; Heb 10:30

Rather than worrying about whether God sees injustice—
we know He does—or whether He is going to act—we know
He will—Christians ought to rest securely in the assurance
that God is just. He will bring ultimate justice to the affairs
of men. His grace, we should strive to end it where we can.
But there will be many injustices we cannot address because they
are far away or in circles of power far above us. Even then, we can
have tremendous peace, knowing that God has it all covered.

How can the Christian not respond in worship? Christians worship Him for His holiness and His righteousness, honor Him for
His goodness and truth, and praise Him for His grace and mercy. It
is only appropriate, too, to worship Him for His sovereign justice.
In His eternal presence in glory, justice will not be an unfortu-
nate thing made necessary by the fall. God's justice will make for
a perfect communion of His people for all eternity. As glorious
as an eternity in His presence beholding His holiness, His goodness, His truth, is an eternity in His presence beholding His justice.

SUMMARY

We have seen how God's justice, sometimes a source of controversy
and to many a source of fear rather than consolation, should be a
comfort and a blessing to God's people. What a blessing to know that
He is perfectly just at all times. We considered some misconceptions
about His justice, that it can be trumped by His love or that even
He answers to a natural law of justice, and found that He remains
sovereign and is the source of all justice. And we examined how we
can imitate God's justice in all of our lives, and finally saw the tremendous peace that is ours, knowing that God's justice will prevail.

CONTEMPLATIONS

↑↓1

Forgive me, Lord, when I try to make You submit to some abstract form of cosmic justice, rather than letting You be God. To do so is to put You in a box, to deny Your sovereignty, to "undeify" You. Perhaps that's why I do it, for if I can hold You against an external standard, I get the upper hand. May I never think this way! Forgive me, too, when I presume upon Your mercy, thinking it is stronger than Your justice. You are wholly consistent with Yourself, Father. Help me to accept and submit to You as You are, not as I wish You to be.

↑↓2

Lord, I know I do not have the same passion for justice You do. When I feel cheated or oppressed, suddenly I am an activist, but I am too, too content to let the poor, the weak, and the powerless fend for themselves. Forgive me, Father. Help me to be more just in my life. Help me to understand, to adhere to, and to uphold Your law, to Your glory, and in the Name of the One who is coming to judge the living and the dead.

↑↓3

Gracious Savior, give me eyes to see the injustice all around me, that I might see the world with Your eyes. But let me not grow impatient or despair. It is my sinful nature that wants what I want when I want it. And I want justice *now*! Except where it relates to my sins. I am such a hypocrite! Forgive me when I deny that You are good even when You delay judgment, for I know in saner moments that You have Your reasons, Your good and perfect reasons. Forgive me, too, when I ignore injustice because it doesn't bear directly on me. Give me a godly heart for the widow and the orphan, the poor and the oppressed. Forgive me when I find them easy to ignore, and when I finally begin to see all of the sin and injustice around me. Lord, help me to trust in You and Your justice, or I will surely be overwhelmed.

Chapter 9

GOD IS TRUTH

Jesus answered, "I am the way and the truth and the life."

John 14:6

Truth is elusive and uncommon in our society. We swim in a sea of half-truths, misrepresentations, and outright lies. Whether we are reading or watching the news, listening to an account of a criminal trial, or listening to an account of a dispute between two spouses, we frequently wonder what *really* happened. We crave the truth, but sometimes, it seems like we will never know.

Many seek to suppress the truth, to avoid a punishment, to gain an advantage, or merely so that they might live as they please. We tell lies of omission, leaving out those parts of a story that make us look bad and hoping no one finds out the whole truth. Or we exaggerate those aspects of a story that make us look good and paint us in the best light. Or we can tell selectively edited stories to make our friends—or the Church—look good and our enemies look bad.

Just as we should not selectively present the truth to make ourselves look good, when we do tell the truth, the whole truth and nothing but the truth, our motive should not be to look really, really good and moral. We should not take credit for our truthfulness or think we are exceptionally good people when we are truthful. Our motivation ought rather to be simply and exclusively to glorify God.

"Teach me Your way, O LORD, that I may walk in Your truth." [220]

Many challenge the very notion of truth itself.

"Then Pilate said to him, 'So you are a king?' Jesus answered, 'You say that I am a king. For this purpose I was born and for this purpose I have come into the world—to bear witness to the truth. Everyone who is of the truth listens to my voice.' Pilate said to him, 'What is truth?'" [221]

But the denial of truth is ultimately not just a philosophical exercise. It is a direct attempt to displace God. The first to question God's truthfulness was Satan, who asked Eve in the garden, "Did God *really* say . . . ?" When Eve affirmed God's words, Satan said, "No." Only when it was too late did Eve realize, "The serpent deceived me." [222] It is no wonder Jesus calls him the "Father of Lies." [223]

Of course, Christians should imitate God in His complete truth, not Satan in his subtle, incomplete misrepresentations. And that means that I have to seek to know and speak and live His truth in my own

220 (God delights in truth) Ps 86:11; 1 Tim 3:15; 2 Tim 2:25; Ps 51:6; Prov 12:17; John 3:21, 14:6; 2 Cor 4:2; Eph 4:15
221 (Jesus is truth) John 18:37-38; 1 John 1:6; John 3:21, 5:32, 14:6, 17:3; Eph 4:15; Rev 3:7, 16:7
222 (Satan is the deceiver) Gen 3:1, 4, 13; 2 Cor 11:3; Eph 6:11; Rev 12:9
223 (Satan is the father of lies) John 8:44; Rev 20:3; 2 Thess 2:9-10; Matt 13:19

life. I need to know truth as God has revealed it in His word. And when I speak, I should only speak the truth. My life, too, should conform to truth. I should be the kind of man sought by Moses:

"Men who fear God, men of truth, who hate dishonest gain." [224]

My actions need to match my speech, especially what I say about God. It is, after all, the truth of God that makes us holy. [225] This also means that, because "true worshippers worship the Father in truth," [226] my worship of Him should be about Him, not me.

↑↓1

TRUTH IS ROOTED IN THE CHARACTER OF GOD

Truth, therefore, has an importance far greater than what it means for us as individuals. God is jealous that the truth come to light and be proclaimed, not just because when truth fails we experience confusion and suffer deception. God values truth because truth is one of His attributes—it's who He is. We ought, ultimately, to be excited about the truth because it reflects the character of God. [227] Truth is such an essential aspect of who God is that He is even called by the name, "True."

---

224 (We should speak truth) Prov 12:17; 1 John 1:6; Ex 18:21, 20:16; Prov 19:5, 9, 21:28, 24:28; Matt 19:18; Deut 19:16-20

225 (The truth of God makes us holy) John 1:14, 17, 14:6, 17:17; 1 Pet 1:16; Ps 71:22; 1 John 1:6, 5:20; 2 Cor 4:2; 2 Thess 2:13

226 (Worship in truth) John 4:23; Ps 145:18; John 1:17; Ps 40:6-8; Is 29:13; Matt 15:7-9; Mark 7:6-7; Phil 3:3; Deut 6:5; Heb 10:22-23

227 (God is truth) Deut 32:4 ; Rom 3:4; 1 John 5:6, 20; John 3:33, 7:28, 8:26, 14:6, 16:13, 17:3; Jer 10:10; Ps 33:4; Is 65:16; 2 Chr 15:3

"Then I saw heaven opened, and behold, a white horse! The one sitting on it is called Faithful and True, and in righteousness He judges and makes war." [228]

That truth is rooted in the character of God resolves the debate about whether or not truth even exists. In a generation that says everything depends on a person's perspective and background and experience, one can stand firm and say there is such a thing as absolute truth.

Because God is truth, it only makes sense that when God speaks, He speaks the truth. The psalmist says, "The sum of Your word is truth." [229] Jesus affirms that God's Word is Truth. And the angel who appeared to John in the book of Revelation said, *"These words are trustworthy and true."* [230] In Genesis, when God made his covenant promises to Abraham, He swore by Himself because there was nothing more true in the universe that He could appeal to. [231]

TRUTH IS NOT FOR THE FAINT OF HEART

But not all of God's truths are simple, easy, and pleasant truths. In particular, the Bible, God's Word, affirms the truth of death and the coming judgment of sin and that salvation can only be found in Jesus Christ. [232] Sinful man argues for a relative universe, a sliding scale of judgment whereby only Adolf Hitler, Joseph Stalin, and most child molesters go to hell because, compared to them, every-

228 (God is called True) Rev 19:11
229 (God speaks truth) Ps 119:160; Ps 119:142, 172; John 1:17, 17:17, 18:37-38; Titus 1:2; 2 Sam 7:28; 2 Tim 2:15; 1 Kin 17:24
230 (The Bible is true) Rev 22:6; John 10:35, 17:17; Prov 30:5; Ps 12:6, 18:30, 19:7, 119:151; 2 Tim 3:16
231 (God swears by Himself) Gen 22:16; Heb 6:13; Is 45:23
232 (The truth of salvation by Christ alone) Acts 4:12, 10:43; Luke 24:47; John 14:6, 20:31; Gal 1:7; Is 45:21-22; Eph 2:18, 5:23; Heb 10:20

one else seems pretty nice.

In the Old Testament, though, God executed judgment of sin through His people, and the Israelites were tasked with killing all of the pagan residents of the Promised Land, even women and children. This is hard for us to accept, but we explain it away by saying that that was then and God has mellowed now and Christ is gracious—where the Lord was wrathful. But:

> *"Jesus Christ is the same yesterday and today and forever."* [233]

and the Apostle Paul reminds us that:

> *"The wages of sin* [all sin] *is* [still] *death,"* [234]

and,

> *"The judgments of the Lord are true and righteous altogether."* [235]

Even among those who acknowledge an eternal judgment awaits us, conventional wisdom (which is no wisdom at all) holds that Buddha, Allah, Krishna, or the Tao can get us "there" as effectively as Christ, even though Scripture says:

> *"There is salvation in no one else; for there is no other name under heaven that has been given among men by which we must be saved,"* [236]

---

233 (Truth does not change) Heb 13:8; Heb 1:12, 6:18; John 8:58; Rev 1:4, 8; James 1:17; Ps 102:25-27; Num 23:19; Mal 3:6; 1 Sam 15:29; Titus 1:2
234 (Sin brings condemnation) Rom 6:23; 2 Pet 3:7; Jude 14-15; Deut 9:7, 28:15-68; Is 13:11, 26:21; Ps 145:20; James 1:15; Gal 6:7
235 (God's judgment is true) Ps 19:9; Ps 97:2, 119:137; Deut 32:4; Rev 19:11-21; James 2:9-11; Gal 3:10; Jude 7
236 (Only Jesus forgives) Acts 4:12, 10:43; Luke 24:47; John 20:31; Gal 1:7

and,

> *"This is eternal life, that they may know You, the only true God, and Jesus Christ whom You have sent."* [237]

Meanwhile:

> *"Those who perish, because they did not receive the love of the truth so as to be saved . . . . They all may be judged who did not believe the truth, but took pleasure in wickedness."* [238]

Those whom God has called into saving relationship with Himself through His Son, those,

> *"God chose . . . as the first fruits to be saved, through sanctification by the Spirit and belief in the truth,"* [239]

and they should not fear, but should welcome every syllable of His holy, most truthful Word. For Christians, saved by God's grace, it is not threats and judgment but promises and hope.

↑↓2

GOD'S TRUTH IS A STRONG SHIELD

In the book of Proverbs, Agur says, "Every word of God proves true; he is a shield to those who take refuge in him." [240] The truth

---

237 (Only Jesus saves) John 17:3; Eph 2:18, 5:23; John 14:6; Heb 10:20

238 (Souls perish outside of Christ) 2 Thess 2:10, 12; Matt 5:22, 13:41-42, 25:46; Rev 19:20, 20:10, 14-15; 2 Thess 1:8-10

239 (The redeemed are saved through the truth) 2 Thess 2:13; 1 Thess 2:13; 2 Thess 2:10; 1 Cor 1:18, 21, 23, 25 2:14; Gal 4:14; John 1:17; 2 Tim 1:9

240 (God speaks truth) Prov 30:5; Ps 25:5, 119:142, 160, 172; John 17:17; Titus 1:2; 2 Sam 7:28; 1 Kin 17:24; Matt 22:16

of God and His word are a comfort beyond merely assuring us that we will not be deceived in this life or judged in the next. God's truth is a shield, a protection, a place of refuge. [241] When all around us gives way, when, as the Irish poet William Butler Yeats described it, "Things fall apart; the centre cannot hold; Mere anarchy is loosed upon the world," [242] we can take refuge in God's eternal Word.

We can take comfort because God is unwaveringly true and His revealed Word is true.

> *"Let God be true though everyone were a liar."* [243] *"It is impossible for God to lie."* [244]

> *"His Mercy is great unto the heavens, and His truth unto the clouds."* [245]

Because God is true and His Word is true, we can know that His promises are reliable to us and sufficient basis for our hope for all eternity. Our destination of heaven is sure, salvation by the blood of Christ is certain, because God has said so, and God is truth. [246]

At the same time, though, God's threats for the lost are equally true. We cannot ignore or be callous to the truths expressed in God's

241 (God's truth is a refuge) Prov 30:5; Ps 3:3, 18:2, 19:14, 28:7, 31:3, 91:2, 4; Jer 16:19
242 Yeats, W.B. "The Second Coming." *The Dial* (1920): n. pag. Print.
243 (God is true) Rom 3:4; Deut 32:4; 1 John 5:6, 20; John 3:33, 7:28, 8:26, 14:6, 16:13; Rev 19:11
244 (God cannot lie) Heb 6:18; 2 Tim 2:13; Titus 1:2; Num 23:19; Mal 3:6; 1 Sam 15:29; 1 Cor 1:9, 10:13; 2 Cor 1:18; Is 49:7
245 (God's truth is beyond our comprehension) Ps 57:10; Job 11:7-9; Ps 139:6, 17-18, 147:5; Is 40:28; Eccl 3:11, 8:17; Rom 11:33; Eph 3:10
246 (God's promises are true) Rom 8:32; 2 Chr 6:10; Is 46:8-11; Rom 4:21; Jer 24:6, 25:12-13, 29:10; Amos 9:15; Acts 13:23; Eph 1:4; Ps 111:7-9

Word about certain destruction for the wicked. Eternal, conscious torment in hell for the damned is real and true and should move us to evangelize.

> *"The Lord is not slow to fulfill His promise as some count slowness, but is patient toward you, not wishing that any should perish, but that all should reach repentance."* [247]

God's Word regarding these things is true, and the reason He communicated this truth to us is that we might share the gospel out of concern for the lost. [248]

The world would say that truth is elusive and variable—a constantly moving target. Because truth is the rooted character of God, though, it is not relative at all. It is absolute. And because of who God is, His truth is absolutely beautiful. How can I not want more of it?

> *"If you abide in my word, you are truly my disciples, and you will know the truth, and the truth will set you free."* [249]

↑↓3

Summary

Our society may consider truth elusive, but we consider it attainable and essential in God. Sometimes, sinful people feel it is important

247 (God's patience toward those not yet redeemed) 2 Pet 3:9; Ps 86:5, 15, 103:3, 130:4, 145:8; Joel 2:13; Mic 7:18; Ex 34:6; Jon 4:2
248 (God's truth motivates us to evangelize) 2 Tim 1:8, 2:10; Eph 3:1, 13; Col 1:24; 1 Cor 13:4, 7; 2 Cor 1:6, 3:12, 7:4
249 (God's truth is freedom) John 8:31-32, 36; Rom 6:18, 22, 8:2; 1 Cor 7:22; 2 Cor 3:17; Gal 5:1, 13; James 1:25, 2:12; 1 Pet 2:16

either to hide truths that reflect poorly on them or to broadcast truths that make them look good. We should imitate God in His truth, though, whether it is pleasant or unpleasant. We must because God is not only truthful, He is truth itself. This means His every word is truthful, including what He says about good and evil. And that is what sinful man also tries to make relative. The denial of truth is, in fact, a direct attempt to displace God. God's people, though, should embrace God's truth, and with it, His standards of good and evil. We should also try to imitate His truthfulness in all of our speech and actions and take comfort from the many true and certain promises in His Word.

CONTEMPLATIONS

↑↓1

Dear Lord God, Father of all that is true and right and just, I am frustrated by the elusiveness of truth. Yet I am guilty of making the truth obscure. Forgive me when I tell selective truths or lies of omission. Forgive me when I distort stories because I don't want to face the consequences of the truth. Show me my foolishness, Lord, when I start to believe my own lies. Forgive me when I try to turn even my truth-telling into being all about me and my virtues on display.

↑↓2

What an amazing thing, God, not just that You are *truthful*, but that You are *truth*. You never lie. You never deceive. What You say will happen because You will make it so, and nothing can stop You. And what You say about right and wrong, good and evil is true, too. Lord, help me accept Your truth, and not the thinking of the world, which is that truth and what is right and wrong change like the seasons. Help me accept those truths that convict me or make me uncomfortable because Your Word is truth, and the injuries it inflicts will heal me in the end.

↑↓3

Lord, give me a zeal for Your truth. Your words are light and life and truth. The more I know of Your Word, the more I know of You. Help me not to doubt or succumb to the spirit of the age, but to rest in You, to delight in Your truth because Your promises are sure. What You say will indeed come to pass. My hope is forever bound up in Christ and His glory. Praise Him. Let me, too, take Your veracious threats to heart, and proclaim salvation in Christ to all who will listen.

Chapter 10

A JEALOUS GOD

"You shall not go after other gods, the gods of the peoples who are around you—for the Lord your God in your midst is a jealous God—lest the anger of the Lord your God be kindled against you, and He destroy you from off the face of the earth."

Deuteronomy 6:14-15

OUR JEALOUSY

We can tend to think of jealousy as a misplaced or petty emotion. We also pervert jealousy, claiming a right that does not belong to us. We can be jealous for what we think is ours, or what we believe should belong to us. We may also be angry because someone we love is liked by someone else, even if he or she doesn't invite or return that affection.

Much of our jealousy stems from our selfishness, ingratitude, and greed, our failure to be content with how God has provided for us.

And this is sin. The tenth commandment illustrates the myriad ways we can want things that are not intended for us, whether they be our neighbor's house or spouse, children, land, material goods, employer, coworkers, life experience, opportunities, *"or anything that is your neighbor's."* [250]

And because we sin this way often, it is very easy for us to assume jealousy is always sinful. Then we both attribute sin to God and impinge upon His character or we deny His jealousy and miss a crucial part of who He is.

↑↓1

JEALOUSY RIGHTLY UNDERSTOOD

In contrast to our perversion, God's jealousy is always perfect and good. God is jealous of what is His—all things—all love and devotion should belong to Him and Him alone. [251] There are numerous examples in the Bible of God's holy jealousy. [252] Virtuous jealousy, jealousy as it should be, as it is demonstrated by God, is a consuming single-minded pursuit of a good end.

God has a right to be jealous over us, whether we see it demonstrated in our lives or not. [253] Not only does He have the right to be jealous, He is jealous, and we need to know this and humbly fear this aspect

---

250 (Our jealousy is sin) Ex 20:17; Mark 7:21-23; Prov 14:30, 23:17, 27:4; Job 5:2; Gal 5:19-21; Rom 13:13; 1 Cor 13:4-7

251 (All devotion belongs to God) Ex 20:4-5, 34:14; Deut 6:13-14; Ps 63:6-8, 69:32, 81:9; Matt 4:9-10; Phil 2:9-11; Rev 4:10-11;

252 (Examples of God's jealousy) Ex 20:5, 34:14; Deut 4:24, 5:9, 32:16; John 24:19; Ps 78:58, 79:5; 1 Cor 10:22; 2 Cor 11:2

253 (God is righteous and jealous) Ps 48:10, 97:2, 6, 111:3, 119:142, 145:17; Is 5:16, 45:21; Job 37:23; Ex 34:14; Josh 24:19

of His nature, for He will not be mocked [254] nor played the fool. God is unapologetically jealous of His chosen people. He declares this again and again throughout Scripture.

It was true of Old Testament Israel:

> "*You are a people holy to the LORD your God. The LORD your God has chosen you to be a people for His treasured possession, out of all the peoples who are on the face of the earth.*" [255]

And it is true of the New Testament Church, which is Christ's bride:

> "*Husbands, love your wives, as Christ loved the church and gave Himself up for her, that he might sanctify her, having cleansed her by the washing of water with the word, so that He might present the church to Himself in splendor, without spot or wrinkle or any such thing, that she might be holy and without blemish.*" [256]

GOD'S JEALOUSY FOR US

So God has established that He has a legitimate, righteous claim on us. He has made us and He has redeemed those He chose; we are His. And this is the source of God's jealousy. For Christians, He is our sovereign Lord by creation and redemption, [257] and He is our loving father by adoption. [258]

---

254 (God is not mocked) Gal 6:7; 1 Cor 6:9; 2 Cor 9:6; Hos 8:7, 10:12; Prov 11:18; Job 4:8

255 (Israel belongs to God) Deut 7:6; Jer 7:23, 11:4, 24:7; Ex 5:1; Lev 26:12; Ps 53:6; Is 52:6; Luke 1:17; Heb 11:25; Rev 21:3; Horton, 86

256 (Christians belong to God) Eph 5:25-27; Eph 5:28-32; John 3:29; Rev 19:7, 21:9, 22:17; Horton, 87

257 (God is sovereign) Ps 47:2, 103:19, 115:3, 135:6; Is 41:4, 43:13, 46:10; Dan 4:17, 35; Rom 9:19-21

258 (God is our Father) 2 Cor 1:3, 6:18; 1 Cor 8:6; Deut 32:6; Ps 68:5, 103:13; Matt 6:26, 7:11; Luke 12:29-31; Prov 3:11-12

But if we behave as if we answer to no one but ourselves, He is justly displeased. [259]

> *"But my people have forgotten me; they make offerings to false gods; they made them stumble in their ways, in the ancient roads, and to walk into side roads, not the highway."* [260]

And His displeasure can turn to righteous anger when we give our love and devotion to another, pretend god. Any such challenge to God's rightful claim provokes His wrath.

> *"Kiss the Son, lest he be angry, and you perish in the way, for His wrath is quickly kindled. Blessed are all who take refuge in Him."* [261]

God is angry because giving our love and devotion to another robs Him of His glory. [262] Only He is the Creator of all things seen and unseen. [263] Only He is all-powerful, all-knowing, ever-present. [264] Only He is the definition of goodness, truth, and beauty. [265] Only He is holy. [266]

---

259 (To forget God is sin) Deut 4:9, 23, 6:10-12, 8:10-14, 9:7-8; Is 51:12-13, 55:6-8; 1 Kin 2:1-4; Judges 8:33-34; Job 8:11-13

260 (Christians belong to God) Jer 18:15; 2 Chr 7:14; Jer 2:32; Hos 1:10

261 (We provoke God's wrath) Ps 2:12; Deut 9:7-8, 32:16; Josh 7:1; Jer 32:30-33; 2 Chr 36:15-16; Hos 12:14; 1 Kin 16:13; 2 Kin 17:11, 22:17; 2 Chr 33:6; Horton, 87

262 (God will not share His glory) Is 42:8, 48:11; Ex 20:4-5, 34:14; Deut 6:13-14; Ps 63:6-8, 69:32, 81:9; Matt 4:9-10; Php 2:9-11; Rev 4:10-11

263 (God is creator) Ps 33:9; Ps 33:6, 148:5-6; Gen 1:3; Acts 17:24; Col 1:16-17; Heb 1:10; Rev 4:11, 10:6, 14:7

264 (God is all powerful, all knowing and everywhere present) Rev 1:8; Job 9:4, 37:16; Is 40:28, 43:13; 1 John 3:20; Ps 139:5, 147:5; Prov 15:3; 1 Kin 8:27

265 (God is good, true, and beautiful) 1 John 1:5; James 1:17; Ps 25:8, 50:2, 86:5, 100:5, 106:1, 119:68; Jer 10:10, 33:11; Gen 1:4; John 7:28, 14:6

266 (God is holy) Rev 15:4, 16:5; Heb 7:26; Ps 16:10, 71:22, 78:41, 89:18; Mark 1:24; Is 5:24, 6:3, 60:9; 2 Kin 19:22; Jer 51:5

And even though we have all transgressed against that holiness, only He has redeemed Christians through the shed blood of His Son. [267] Only He is worthy of our attention and devotion, and only He deserves the glory we may give to our idols or reserve for ourselves. And when we do that, He is justifiably jealous of the honor, glory, and praise we deny Him.

Several chapters from now, we will discuss God's wrath and see how God's anger at being slighted by His rebellious creation is not fully completed in His disposition of jealousy. He is so sinned against, so offended, and so just, that His jealousy is ultimately realized in His holy wrath when He brings Divine and terrible judgment on those creatures who rebel against Him and who are not covered by the blood of His Son.

Don't minimize the justness of His jealousy. Don't paint all jealousy as petty and sinful. God has the right to be unhappy about the love we deny Him, and He is angry when we show devotion to another. We can incur God's jealousy by being ourselves jealous of something other than Him. We all have priorities in life, and we all have ultimate priorities. Which do we defend? Of which are we jealous when they are violated? If we are jealous for the wrong thing, we will not be jealous for the right thing. We will have created a false priority, which, as we have seen, might even rise to the level of idolatry in our lives. [268]

In doing this, we behave as if we are free moral agents and as if we ourselves determine who or what we will love and serve and worship. We downplay God's sovereignty and overstate any claim

---

267 (Jesus redeems) John 10:11, 17, 15:13; Rom 4:26, 5:6-8; Eph 5:2; 1 John 3:16, 4:9-10; Matt 20:28; Mark 10:45

268 (Human jealousy is idolatry and sin) Deut 5:9; Gen 29:31, 30:1; James 4:2; Num 5:14-15; Ps 37:1-3; Acts 7:9; Eph 5:3; Gal 5:19-21; Rom 13:13

we might have even to our own affections. We are so hypocritical that we claim God is small if He cannot permit us outside interests when, really, we are just as jealous in our human relationships.

↑↓2

IMITATING GOD'S JEALOUSY

And yet, if we are in Christ and guided by His Holy Spirit, there is an entirely appropriate way in which we might imitate His jealousy. We must be jealous for the same things He is. We can long for His kingdom, [269] and we can be zealous for His character to be manifest in our lives and relationships. [270]

> *"I feel a divine jealousy for you, since I betrothed you to one husband, to present you as a pure virgin to Christ."* [271]

We can also be jealous for God's honor, His glory. Are we offended when we hear people disrespecting God or even speaking blasphemy? Jealousy is more than an option in such instances; it is the only right response. [272] Can we hear the Lord we love being maligned and have it not bother us? Or is our ire more easily aroused at hearing our favorite sports team be disrespected than the holy God of the universe? If so, we are not being jealous for God's honor and

269 (Christians long for God's kingdom) Matt 8:21-22, 13:44-46; Luke 9:61-62; Php 1:23, 3:13; Ps 45:10; John 14:3; 2 Cor 5:8; 1 Thess 4:17
270 (Christians should be zealous for sanctification) 1 Cor 12:31, 14:1, 16:14; Lev 19:2, 20:7-8; Heb 2:11; 1 Pet 1:15-16; 1 Thess 4:3; 2 Thess 2:13; Eph 1:4; 1 Cor 1:2
271 (Christians should be zealous for a pure church) 2 Cor 11:2; Mal 3:3; Acts 15:9; James 4:8; 1 Pet 1:22; Ezra 6:20; 1 Cor 5:13; 2 Cor 7:1; 1 John 3:3
272 (Christians hate blasphemy) Ps 73:9, 74:18; Is 52:5; Mal 3:13; 2 Thess 2:4; Rom 1:28-32, 2:24; 1 Tim 1:13, 20; Rev 13:1

His glory. Of course, we must be wise in our responses, but if we simply shrug off such words, it's a fair question to ask ourselves how deep our love for God really goes.

Another way we can be jealous in imitation of God is if we are jealous for His image in man. God told Noah the punishment for homicide is execution because in killing a man, one doesn't just kill the man but also murders the image of God in that man. Similarly, abortion does not just murder an unborn innocent but takes the life of one created in God's image. Christ even teaches in the Sermon on the Mount that in slandering another person, we fail to honor him or her as an image bearer of God, so we will be subject to judgment. [273]

↑↓3

GOD'S JEALOUSY FOR CHRISTIANS

Christians are not only witnesses and imitators of God's jealousy, but they are also objects of His jealousy. God is jealous for His honor and glory, but He is also jealous for us, His people. We are His prized possession, [274] His bride whom He loves. That makes us an ultimate priority for Him and something special in His sight, and as such, He will defend us jealously.

> *"Then the LORD became jealous for His land and had pity on His people."* [275]

---

273 (Christians should be zealous for the image of God in man) Gen 9:6; James 3:9; Ex 5:17; Matt 5:22, 19:18; Deut 19:11-13; Gen 1:26; 2 Cor 4:4; Heb 1:3

274 (Christians belong to God) Deut 26:18; Gal 3:26, 29; Luke 3:8; 1 Pet 2:9; Col 3:12; 1 Thess 1:4; 2 Thess 2:13; Eph 1:5; Titus 2:14

275 (God will defend us) Joel 2:18; Ex 34:24; 2 Chr 32:7; Neh 4 and 9; 1 John 5:18; John 17:12; 2 Thess 3:3; Jude 24; Eph 3:20

Because He is jealous for us, He is sure to watch over us, and we need not fear being forgotten or neglected. We are watched over tenderly and protectively by God's jealousy. He will not share His honor or His glory with anyone, and He will not share His prized possession once He takes us as His own. We can have tremendous comfort in knowing that the Lord will suffer no rivals and will watch over, protect, keep, and defend us as His chosen people until the end.

The cross of Christ serves as the greatest illustration of this fact, for in His death and resurrection, Christ defeated even death when it thought it had a hold on His people. [276] Praise Him for His death and resurrection. Praise Him for His steadfast love and care. Praise Him for His jealousy.

↑↓4

SUMMARY

We have seen how we view jealousy incorrectly, as a fault rather than a virtue. For us, this is true because it involves passion for a right that is not truly ours. But God deserves all honor, glory, praise, and allegiance, and so, His jealousy is appropriate. We looked at examples of sinful, human jealousy and righteous, Divine jealousy. We examined reasons for God's jealousy and looked at how we should respond to His holy jealousy. We also discussed how it is appropriate for us as God's children to imitate His jealousy as we strive to imitate all of His perfect attributes. We imitate His holy and good jealousy by defending His sovereignty and calling out idolatry when we see it. Finally, we contemplated the most glorious manifestation of God's jealousy—His wholehearted

---

276 (Christ's death is greatest example of God's jealousy for us) 1 Cor 15:25-26, 54-55; 2 Tim 1:10; Rev 20:14, 21:4; Eph 5:2; Rom 4:25, 5:18; Is 53:10

devotion to His bride, Christ's Church, and the marvelous benefits we, as His people, derive from this benevolent, virtuous attribute.

CONTEMPLATIONS

↑↓1

Lord, how often am I upset because something I think should be mine belongs to someone else? I am sure it is a bigger problem even than I am aware of. I think of Cain, I think of Jonah, both of whom You asked, "Are you right to be angry?" We read their stories and they seem so oblivious to their own sins, to the very principles of right and wrong, but I know that is me, too. Forgive me. Show me my sinful, covetous heart so that I can repent and find my satisfaction in You alone.

↑↓2

Gracious Heavenly Father, how often have I provoked You to jealousy by taking the love I should have for You and giving it to something else. Forgive me, Lord, I pray! Nothing else is worthy, nothing else deserves the ultimate affection reserved for You alone. Yet even in my rebellion, You have been gracious. Your response to my wayward heart has been to love me even more, love me to the point of death, even death on the cross. Too often I think of the cross as a judicial necessity, but to see it as the act of a jealous suitor doing what it takes to win the heart of his love—what passion! What love! What grace!

↑↓3

Lord God, forgive me, for I know I do a miserable job of imitating Your jealousy. I deny that You have a right to be upset, when You alone determine what is true and right. I make apologies for You to those who would question Your anger at having just claim when all You have made is violated. And I may be upset by insults to my flag, while blasphemies heaped upon Your holy name only elicit a shrug. I believe man is created in Your image, but my callousness to the killing all around me denies this belief by its lack of outrage. Make me jealous for the things that make You jealous. Help me to see the justness of Your claim and the depth of Your love. A right understanding of Your perfect holy jealousy will be the only right result.

↑↓4

What? The God of the Universe, the Creator and Sustainer of all things, the Gracious Redeemer of men is jealous for . . . me? What an amazing truth. I may not feel that special most days, but that does not stop You from lavishing Your love and affection on me and all believers, nor from Your jealousy being provoked when we do not love You as we should. By Your grace, for Your glory, Father, bind my heart to yours that it may never wander. Help me to see afresh and anew each and every day Your love demonstrated at the cross and how just Your claim and how sincere Your devotion. I love You, Lord; help my lack of love.

Chapter 11

WHAT IS MAN?

"What is man that You are mindful of him, and the son of man that
You care for him? Yet You have made him a little lower than the
heavenly beings and crowned him with glory and honor.
You have given him dominion over the works of Your hands;
You have put all things under His feet."

Psalm 8:4-6

In a book that strives to be as God-centered as possible, it may
seem odd to include a chapter on man. But in the words of the
famous theologian John Calvin:

> Our wisdom, in so far as it ought to be deemed true and solid
> wisdom, consists almost entirely of two parts: the knowledge
> of God and of ourselves. [277]

---

277 Calvin, Jean. *Institutes of Christian Religion*. Geneva: n.p., 1536. Print.

CREATED IN GOD'S IMAGE

Man's first appearance in Scripture is at his creation by God. We did not create ourselves. There is no such thing as a "self-made" man. [278] We are dependent on Him for our very existence. [279] This should humble our sinful pride, but it doesn't seem to. People often try to deny God's creative work and would rather say that man is a product of chance evolution than have to answer to a creator.

It is significant not just *that* we were created but also *how*. Before He created Adam, God said, "*Let us make man in our image after our likeness.*" [280] The Lord was deliberate in His choice of the word "image." In making man, He did not replicate Himself, nor are we little gods. [281] We are not all-knowing, for example. We are, however, made with a special capacity similar to God's in that we can exercise several of His attributes, such as holiness, goodness, justice, and truth.

And once He created humankind, God looked at His creation and said, "It is very good." [282] And when He created Adam and Eve, God also said:

> "*Let them have dominion over the fish of the sea and over the birds of the heavens and over the livestock and over all the earth and over every creeping thing that creeps on the earth.*" [283]

278 (God is our creator) Gen 1:1, 26, 2:23; Ps 33:6, 9, 90:2; John 1:3; Col 1:16; Rev 4:11, 10:6; Acts 17:24-25; Is 45:18; Heb 11:3
279 (Mankind is dependent on God) Matt 4:4, 5:45; 1 Cor 3:7; Acts 14:17, 17:24-25; Lev 26:4; Deut 8:3, 11:14; Ps 147:8; Jer 17:5; John 4:34
280 (God created mankind) Gen 1:26; Gen 5:1, 9:6; 1 Cor 11:7; James 3:9; John 1:3; Col 1:16; Rev 4:11; Ps 100:3, 139:13
281 (God alone is God) Ex 15:11; 1 Sam 2:2; Is 40:18, 25, 44:6, 45:5-6; 1 Tim 6:15-16; Mark 2:7; 1 Kin 8:23; 2 Chr 6:24; Jer 10:6
282 (God created everything good) Gen 1:4, 10, 12, 18, 21, 25, 31; Eccl 7:29; 1 Tim 4:4
283 (Mankind is given dominion) Gen 1:26, 28, 9:1-3; Ps 8:6; Dan 4:17, 25, 32; Jer 27:5; Ps 115:16

Adam and Eve were also created to be relational and to have a relationship with one another, "male and female He created them." [284] They were also to have a relationship with God and to have fellowship and communion with Him just like there is love and relationship within the three persons of the trinity. [285]

THE FALL

But Adam and Eve rebelled against God's authority in the garden, and instead of being satisfied with simply being like Him, they tried to become *equal* with Him. They disobeyed His command and fell from His grace, breaking their perfect fellowship with Him. Understanding this "Fall" is crucial for us today since it is the tragic legacy we all live under. [286]

The Fall changes and does injury to the image of God in man. It harms our relationship with God, with one another, and with creation. Adam and Eve used to walk with God in the cool of the day, but after they sinned, they feared God and hid from Him. [287] When He found them, He cursed them for their sin. To the woman first, He said:

> *"I will greatly multiply your pain in childbirth, in pain you will bring forth children; yet your desire will be for your husband, and he will rule over you." [288]*

284 (Mankind is relational) Gen 1:27, 13:8; Ps 133:1; Mark 12:29-31; Matt 7:12, 22:37-39; Luke 6:31; Heb 13:1; Rom 12:10; 1 Thess 4:9; 1 Pet 1:22
285 (God is relational) Jer 3:14, 31:32; Is 54:5; Hos 3:1; Eph 5:25-32; John 16:27; Rom 8:15-16; Matt 6:9, 7:9-11; 1 John 3:1
286 (Fall of Mankind) Gen 3:1-7
287 (Effects of the Fall) Gen 3:8; Eccl 9:3; Jer 13:23, 17:9; Mark 7:21-23; John 3:19; Rom 8:7-8; 1 Cor 2:14; Eph 4:17-19; 1 John 5:19
288 (Effects of the Fall for women) Gen 3:16

Then to the man, He said:

> *"Cursed is the ground because of you; in toil you will eat of it all the days of your life. Both thorns and thistles it shall grow for you; and you will eat the plants of the field. By the sweat of your face you will eat bread, till you return to the ground, because from it you were taken; for you are dust, and to dust you shall return." [289]*

Mercifully, He did not destroy them forever. And God expelled them from the garden so that they no longer saw His face. The curse also promised strife between the husband and wife and between the descendants of the first couple. [290]

A true, historic, time-space Fall from God's grace best describes human life as we experience it. Created in His image, we have a sense of right and wrong, of justice and truth. But only the Fall explains man's every vice in opposition to Godly virtue—our violence, lies, lust, deception, rage, and hate.

> *"Lord, You made men upright, but they have sought out many devices." [291]*

That these things bother us is further proof that we are created to be otherwise, yet the fact that they continue means we are not as we should be.

To resolve this contrast between what we think life should be and what it is—this conflict between who we are and what we should

---

289 (Effects of the Fall for men) Gen 3:17-19
290 (Relational effects of the Fall) Gen 3:16; James 4:1-4; John 15:19, 17:14; 1 John 2:15; Luke 6:13, 26; Matt 6:24; Rom 6:16
291 (Effects of the Fall) Eccl 7:29; 2 Chr 6:36; 1 Kin 8:46; Job 15:14-16; Rom 3:9-12; James 3:8; Prov 20:9; Eph 2:1-2, 4:17-19; Titus 3:3

be—we look to the God who made us. As respected theologian John Calvin described it:

> Every man, being stung by the consciousness of his own unhappiness, in this way necessarily obtains at least some knowledge of God. Thus, our feeling of ignorance, vanity, want, weakness, in short, depravity and corruption, reminds us, that in the Lord, and none but He, dwell the true light of wisdom, solid virtue, exuberant goodness.
>
> We are accordingly urged by our own evil things to consider the good things of God; and, indeed, we cannot aspire to Him in earnest until we have begun to be displeased with ourselves. [292]

The Apostle Paul begins his letter to the Roman church with a description of just how deep and profound is the problem of human sin.

> *"None is righteous, no, not one; no one understands; no one seeks for God. All have turned aside; together they have become worthless; no one does good, not even one. Their throat is an open grave; they use their tongues to deceive.*
>
> *"The venom of asps is under their lips. Their mouth is full of curses and bitterness. Their feet are swift to shed blood; in their paths are ruin and misery, and the way of peace they have not known. There is no fear of God before their eyes."* [293]

These words are true. They describe us and should humble us and make us ashamed.

---

292 Calvin, Jean. *Institutes of Christian Religion*. Geneva: n.p., 1536. Print.
293 (Depravity of Mankind) Rom 3:10-18; 2 Chr 6:36; Ps 130:3,143:2; Prov 20:9; Eccl 7:20, 29; Is 53:6, 64:6; Rom 3:9-12

↑↓1

But there are many who don't view the Bible as true and are offended by such a low view of humankind. They like to think they are doing okay and that their behavior is normal and acceptable. They like to think more highly of themselves than they ought. As Protagoras of Abdera (ca. 490-ca.420 BC) said, "Of all things the measure is man, of the things that are, that they are, and of the things that are not, that they are not."

Even in Christian circles, such thinking often holds sway because we too often conform to the culture. So we view our sins in terms of "nobody's perfect." We measure man against man (rather than against God) and believe we don't look so bad. As long as I'm a little more virtuous, a little less wicked than the next guy, I can even feel pretty good about myself. But "better than the next guy" is not our standard. Our standard for what is true and good and holy is the Lord Himself, who is truth and goodness and holiness. [294]

SLAVES OF SIN

The legacy we have inherited from the Fall is that we are fallen creatures with a fallen nature to our core. Our situation is very grave.

Apart from the grace of God, there is no fix to our fallen nature. We cannot change it on our own by reading a self-help book or making a New Year's resolution. It's not a matter of simply adopting the right system or believing strongly enough in the power of our dreams. We cannot conjure up enough positive thinking to change the core of what and who we are.

---

294 (God is the holy standard) Rom 3:20, 23, 7:7, 12; 1 John 2:4, 3:4; Is 33:22, 55:6-8; 1 Tim 1:8-10; Luke 16:17; Ps 19:7-9

Scripture plainly teaches us that left to ourselves, we do not just make poor choices out of habit—we *willfully* choose our own destruction. We are bound to do so because we are slaves of sin. Our wills are not our own but the power of sin within us, the so-called "enemy within," compels and controls us. [295]

> *"For whatever overcomes a person, to that he is enslaved."* [296]

> *"I see in my members another law waging war against the law of my mind and making me captive to the law of sin that dwells in my members."* [297]

> *"For the mind that is set on the flesh is hostile to God, for it does not submit to God's law; indeed, it cannot."* [298]

Scripture presents in these passages the image of man being an enslaved captive to sin. Man is not just inclined to sin because of bad examples and bad habits, but man is an actual slave to sin, compelled to sin, lacking the freedom to do otherwise. This doctrine is hard for many people to digest because we like to feel we are not only capable but also free to do as we please.

Those outside of a saving relationship with Jesus Christ, however, are in no way free. They are even more thoroughly and powerfully enslaved because they are enslaved and they don't know it.

> *"By nature we are darkened in our understanding, excluded from the life of God because of the ignorance that is in us, be-*

---

295 Lundgaard, Kris. *The Enemy Within: Straight Talk about the Power and Defeat of Sin.* Phillipsburg, NJ: P & R, 1998. Print.
296 (Slaves to sin) 2 Pet 2:19; Gal 5:17; James 4:1
297 (Captive to sin) Rom 7:23; 1 Cor 2:14; 2 Tim 2:26
298 (Slaves to sin) Rom 8:7; John 8:34; Titus 3:3

cause of the hardness of our hearts." [299]

They are blind, deaf, and foolish.

"Seeing they do not see, and hearing they do not hear, nor do they understand." [300]

They completely lack spiritual understanding.

"The natural person does not accept the things of the Spirit of God, for they are folly to him, and he is not able to understand them because they are spiritually discerned." [301]

"They are 'wise'—in doing evil! But how to do good they know not." [302]

"As a well keeps its water fresh, so she keeps fresh her evil." [303]

They are bound not only to a corrupt and sinful nature, but wittingly or unwittingly, they serve and follow Satan.

"You are of your father the devil, and your will is to do your father's desires. He was a murderer from the beginning, and does not stand in the truth, because there is no truth in him. When he lies, he speaks out of his own character, for he is a liar and the father of lies." [304]

---

299 (Unbelievers are slaves to sin) Eph 4:18, NASB; Eph 2:1-2; 2 Tim 2:25-26; 1 John 3:10, 5:19; John 8:34, 44; Rom 6:20; Titus 3:3

300 (Unbelievers are ignorant) Matt 13:13; Deut 29:4; Jer 5:21; Ezek 12:2

301 (God chooses to reveal Himself) 1 Cor 2:14; Rom 11:8; 2 Cor 3:14, 4:4; Is 42:19-20

302 (Unbelievers are foolish) Jer 4:22

303 (Unbelievers pursue evil) Jer 6:7; Is 57:20; Col 3:5; Prov 21:20, 24:8-9; 2 Pet 2:18; Rom 1:26; Ps 36:4, 140:2; Nah 1:11

304 (Unbelievers follow Satan) John 8:44; Acts 5:1-9, 13:10; 1 John 3:8-10, 5:19; Luke 22:3; John 6:70, 7:7, 13:2; Rev 13:1-8

"When a man's folly brings his way to ruin, his heart rages against the Lord." [305]

Even a Christian, as a sinful, fallen human being, is inclined to rebellion. Our flesh still says, *"We do not want this man to reign over us,"* [306] and *"Who is the LORD that we should obey His voice?"* [307] We are bent on turning away from Him. [308]

↑↓2

War Against Our Sin And Our Flesh

But praise God that He has redeemed the Christian from slavery to sin and makes him instead a slave to *righteousness*. Yes, we go from serving a cruel, evil, tyrannical master who cares nothing for our wellbeing and is content to use us up, to serving a gracious, benevolent master who wants only our good—but we still serve a master. [309] So Christians are slaves of a new Master, servants of God rather than the devil. And His command for us is not to forget or to ignore our former way of life but to wage all-out war against it because although it may no longer have power over us, its influence still persists. [310]

Even once we are living in His kingdom and feel the peace of forgiveness and the hope of glory, we continue to sin and fail daily. An individual's behavior may improve and in some cases improve

---

305 (Unbelievers rage against God) Prov 19:3; Num 14:11; Ps 78:32; Acts 14:2; Heb 4:2; 2 Cor 4:4; John 9:39-41; 1 Tim 1:13; Rev 21:8
306 (Mankind fights the Kingship of God) Luke 19:14
307 (Pharaoh fights the Kingship of God) Ex 5:2
308 (Mankind proclaims himself king) John 3:19-20; 2 Thess 2:4; Acts 5:4; Rom 8:7-8; John 8:44; Is 53:6; Hos 11:7; 2 Tim 2:25-26; Prov 21:10
309 (God is our Master) Rev 1:8, 11:17, 16:14, 21:22; Matt 6:24; Rom 1:20; Is 9:6, 43:13, 49:26, 60:16; Gen 49:24; Deut 10:17
310 (Believers should stand firm in their faith) Matt 10:22, 24:12-13; Phil 2:12-13

drastically, but still none meet His standard of holy perfection. This is unacceptable to the Almighty.

Of course, this doesn't mean that Christian salvation is somehow deficient or that it can be lost. [311] It means that salvation is not a one-time remedy. The Christian must forever abide in Christ and wage war against the flesh in the strength that God provides. Praise Him that we do not fight alone! But fight on we must.

↑↓3

The Apostle Paul gives us a clear picture of what this battle looks like:

"For the desires of the flesh are against the Spirit, and the desires of the Spirit are against the flesh, for these are opposed to each other, to keep you from doing the things you want to do." [312]

And he teaches that this conflict is not one in which we remain passive but characterizes a lifelong struggle, a war even.

"For though we walk in the flesh, we are not waging war according to the flesh." [313]

The Apostle Peter continues the idea that the Christian life is one of struggle against our sinful nature:

"Beloved, I urge you as sojourners and exiles to abstain from the passions of the flesh, which wage war against your soul." [314]

311 (God keeps our faith secure) Luke 22:31-32; Php 3:12-14; 1 Tim 4:16
312 (Fight to follow God) Gal 5:17, 6:9; 2 Pet 1:10-11
313 (Stand firm) 2 Cor 10:3; 1 Cor 16:13-14
314 (Fight against the sinful nature) 1 Pet 2:11; 2 John 9; Rev 14:12

And Paul gives the solution:

"Walk by the Spirit, and you will not gratify the desires of the flesh." [315]

We must submit to our new Master and forsake the old one.

"Those who live according to the flesh set their minds on the things of the flesh, but those who live according to the Spirit set their minds on the things of the Spirit." [316]

"Put on the Lord Jesus Christ, and make no provision for the flesh, to gratify its desires." [317]

"Do not be slothful in zeal, be fervent in spirit, serve the Lord." [318]

Spiritual warfare is a cause to be taken seriously for Scripture is filled with warnings to those who are lazy, unfruitful, and unproductive. The lazy servant is stripped of all he has and cast out. [319] The unfruitful fig tree is cut down and burned. [320] And the vine that produces bad fruit is forsaken and destroyed. [321]

315 (Walk in the Spirit to defeat the flesh) Gal 5:16; Gal 5:24-25; Rom 13:14; Col 1:10-11
316 (Walk in the Spirit to defeat the flesh) Rom 8:5; Matt 16:24; Luke 9:23; Eph 5:8; 1 John 2:6
317 (Remain with God to defeat the flesh) Rom 13:14; Gal 3:27; Rom 6:3; John 15:4; Rev 21:3-4
318 (Serve God to defeat the flesh) Rom 12:11; Eph 4:24, 5:18; Col 3:10; Ps 37:34, 119:3
319 (Our struggle is against the enemy) Eph 6:12; 2 Cor 10:3-4; Rom 13:12-14
320 (Spiritual warfare) Zech 4:6; Gal 5:17; 1 Pet 2:11; 2 Tim 2:3
321 (Stand firm) Is 5:5-6; Rom 7:23; Luke 22:31-32; 2 Tim 3:12; Eph 6:13

It is because this tension exists and because we are at war that meditation as we present it in this book is so important. Our natural inclinations are to sin. The world tells us not to think too deeply, but to follow our hearts, to go with the flow.

But it is only by seeking God and giving careful consideration to His ways that we see the sinfulness of following our own hearts and the contrasting beauty of His heart. When this realization dawns on us, we are moved to obey. [322]

We obey not just because we are compelled by guilt, but we obey because of God's very attractiveness. We are moved to do more than just passively acquiesce; we are roused to fight for the cause of our Lord and Master!

↑↓4

SUMMARY

We have spent some time examining ourselves so that we might better understand the God who made us and saves us. We know that we are created; we have not made ourselves or come into being by chance. We are also created in God's image, which explains our sense of glory and of right and wrong. Sadly, though, all of our lives are colored by the fact that we are fallen from God's grace and desperately sinful. We use ourselves as the standard of righteousness rather than God, and we try to operate independently of Him, even though once saved, we are slaves not to sin but to righteousness. As slaves of righteousness, we war against our flesh with the strength provided by God through His Holy Spirit.

322 (The love of God moves us to obey) Luke 7:47; 2 Cor 5:14-15; John 13:34, 15:16; 1 John 2:10, 3:16, 4:9-11, 19-21; Lev 19:18; Rom 13:8; Col 3:14

CONTEMPLATIONS

↑↓1

Lord, I know I do not appreciate the utter sinfulness of my sin. I am afraid for You to show me and not only because it would destroy my illusions that I am doing okay. I am afraid to know the depth of my sin because the knowledge would completely break me. Yet I repent of what I know. Remind me that, however great and deep and wide and pervasive is my sin, the blood of Christ covers it all. Show me more of my sin so that I might know more of His glory and saving grace. Destroy my illusions of self so that I may rest more fully and surely on Him.

↑↓2

I know I make myself the standard of right behavior. But I also know I don't live up to the standard I hold others to. That makes me wicked and a hypocrite. Forgive me, Lord. Show me the one true standard of right human behavior: the standard set by Christ, who was perfectly obedient to Your high, holy standard. Compared to Him, I know I am utterly wicked and a total failure. But I know that because of His perfect obedience, I am saved. Praise Him! To be found in Christ, to be saved by His grace, to be cleansed by His blood, makes me more holy and righteous than I could ever have hoped to have obtained by my own efforts. Thank You, Lord. And though society tries to press me into its mold, tries to conform me to its thinking, never let me forget my sin and Christ's salvation.

↑↓3

I know my desire to be a free moral agent, to make my own choices, right or wrong, is not unique to me. It is as old as Adam and Eve who wanted to be on par with God, to live and move in His universe without having to answer to Him. I confess how strong this desire is in me. Forgive me, Lord, for this desire. Help me to accept, willingly and eagerly, my role as Your humble servant. As a slave of Your righteousness, let me serve righteousness joyfully. And humble me when that stubborn, independent streak rears its head. If I found myself truly independent for one second, I would no doubt dive headlong into my own destruction. You have saved me, Lord; continue saving me from sin and from myself. Teach me to serve only You.

↑↓4

I know I don't fight my sinful nature the way I should. I often give in to temptation without a fight. Sometimes, I don't even treat it like a fight where my soul is the battleground. I know that Christ accomplished my salvation at the cross, and I leave it at that. If I sin, His blood will cover it, so no big deal. Forgive me, Lord, for that is an awfully callous way for me to treat the blood of my sovereign! He died for me! The least I can do is resist the things He hates. And if I do, I can only fight by His strength, not my own, so I need not fear. Forgive me when I do not pray, when I do not appeal to Your Word, and when I do not enlist Your help and treat spiritual warfare as real.

Chapter 12

THE WRATH OF GOD

"Thus let us offer to God acceptable worship,
with reverence and awe, for our God is a consuming fire."

Hebrews 12:28-29

GOD'S WRATH IS HIS ETERNAL CONTEMPT FOR ALL UNRIGHTEOUSNESS

Mine eyes have seen the glory of the coming of the Lord. He is trampling out the vintage where the grapes of wrath are stored. He hath loosed the fateful lightning of His terrible swift sword. His truth is marching on. [323]

Was this merely a battle hymn of the Union armies invading the South during the U.S. Civil War, or does this verse also represent biblical truth regarding God's coming wrath?

---

323 (The final judgment) Matt 16:27, 25:31, 24:30, 26:64; Luke 2:30, 3:6; Acts 1:11

"And then the sign of the Son of Man will appear in the sky, and then all the tribes of the earth will mourn, and they will see the SON OF MAN COMING ON THE CLOUDS OF THE SKY *with power and great glory. And He will send forth His angels with* A GREAT TRUMPET *and* THEY WILL GATHER TOGETHER *His elect from the four winds, from one end of the sky to the other."* [324]

"So the angel swung his sickle to the earth and gathered the clusters from the vine of the earth, and threw them into the great wine press of the wrath of God." [325]

"Near is the great day of the LORD, near and coming very quickly; listen, the day of the LORD! In it the warrior cries out bitterly. A day of wrath is that day, a day of trouble and distress, a day of destruction and desolation, a day of darkness and gloom, a day of clouds and thick darkness, a day of trumpet and battle cry against the fortified cities and the high corner towers." [326]

"Into Your hand I commit my spirit; You have ransomed me, O LORD, God of truth." [327]

Many people don't believe God is wrathful at all. Undoubtedly, when some hear the mention of God's wrath—if they do believe—they resent Him for it. "How can a God who is love also be wrathful?" they ask.

And some who agree with the truth that God is wrathful, never-

---

324 (Christ's coming) Matt 24:30-31 NASB; John 1:51, 12:14-15; Dan 7:10, 13; Zech 14:5
325 (God's wrath) Rev 14:19 NASB; Rev 19:15; Rom 1:18; John 3:36; Isa 26:21
326 (God's judgment) Zeph 1:14-16 NASB; 1 Thess 1:10; 1 Sam 2:10; Luke 12:5; John 15:6
327 (God's wrath on the cross) Ps 31:5 NASB; Is 53:5-6; 1 Pet 2:24; Gen 3:15; Rom 4:25; Matt 26:39, 42; 1 John 2:2; Eph 1:7; Col 1:14

theless make excuses for Him or feel the need to apologize for this part of who He is. Some think that if He was wrathful, then that was the "Old God," long ago from the Old Testament past, and that He has changed, *matured*. Some, on the other hand, prefer just not to think about it. And some, even among those who believe in God, consider the thought too terrifying to be something worth seriously thinking about or meditating on. [328]

↑↓1

Regardless of what one thinks, we should look at what God's Holy Scriptures say. [329] We don't have to read far in the Bible to find that God makes no attempt to hide His wrath. He is not ashamed to announce that vengeance and fury belong to Him. His own challenge is:

> *"See now that I, even I, am He, and there is no god beside me; I kill and I make alive; I wound and I heal; and there is none that can deliver out of my hand. For I lift up my hand to heaven and swear, As I live forever, if I sharpen my flashing sword and my hand takes hold on judgment, I will take vengeance on my adversaries and will repay those who hate me."* [330]

The wrath of God is His eternal contempt for all unrighteousness. It is His displeasure and indignation against evil. It is the holiness of God actively applied against sin. God is angry against sin because it is a rebellion against His authority, a denial of and an insult to His

---

328 (God is wrathful) Ps 2:11, 33:8; Prov 10:24, 15:33, 16:6; Mal 2:4-6, Php 2:12; Heb 10:31, Rev 21:8; Eccl 8:13
329 (God's word is truth) Ps 12:6, 18:30, 119:151, 160, 172; Prov 30:5; John 17:17; 2 Tim 3:16; Heb 4:12; Rom 15:4; 2 Pet 1:20-21
330 (God doesn't hide His wrath) Deut 32:39-41; Rom 1:18, 2:5; Ps 7:12, 110:5; Is 27:1, 34:5, 66:16; Ezek 21:9-10

unassailable sovereignty. [331] Rebels against God's government will, without a doubt, be made to know that God is the Lord. They will be made to feel the greatness of the Majesty that they despise, and they will experience the dreadfulness of the wrath that He has threatened, that they have disregarded.

This does not mean that God's anger is about petty revenge or malicious retaliation, inflicting injury for the sake of it, or in return for an injury or insult suffered. No, God is never vindictive like we, in our pettiness and sin, can be, but He will vindicate His dominion as the governor of the universe. The day is coming when the Lord will vindicate His majesty, exercise His awful dominion, magnify His justice, and overthrow the proud rebels who have dared to defy Him. [332]

↑↓2

HIS WRATH IS PART OF HIS PERFECTION

When we acknowledge that God is wrathful, we should not think of it as His less glorious dark side. There is no imperfection or fault in God's character. And there is no perfection in Him that is less perfect than another. Therefore, God's wrath is as much a divine perfection as are His love, faithfulness, grace, or mercy. Furthermore, as counterintuitive as it seems, God's character would be diminished, less glorious, even defective if His wrath was missing! [333] Indifference to sin is a moral blemish. How could He who is

---

331 (God is sovereign) Ps 135:6; Is 14:24, 46:10; Dan 4:17, 35; Rom 9:19-21; Job 42:2; 1 Sam 2:10; 2 Chron 20:6

332 (God will punish sin) Jude 1:14-15; Deut 9:7, 28:15-68; Is 13:11, 26:21; Rom 2:5-6, 12; Ps 98:9; Acts 17:31; James 5:9; 2 Pet 3:7

333 (Wrath is consistent with God's character) Rom 1:18; John 3:36; Rev 19:11-21; Nah 1:2-6; Ps 97:2, 119:137, 145:17; Deut 32:4; Job 37:23

infinitely holy ignore sin and refuse to unleash His wrath? How could He who delights only in what is pure and lovely not loathe and hate what is impure and vile? The very nature of God makes hell as real as heaven. [334] Nineteenth century Scottish clergyman Robert Haldane explains this concept as follows:

> God's wrath was revealed when the sentence of death was initially pronounced, when the earth was cursed, and man was driven out of the earthly paradise. [335] It was repeated later in such examples of punishment as the Flood [336] and the destruction of Sodom and Gomorrah by fire from heaven. [337] It is especially revealed, though, in the reign of death throughout the world. [338] It was proclaimed in the curse of the law on every sin, [339] and was the reason for the institution of the sacrificial system. [340]

> In Romans 8, the Apostle Paul points out that all of creation has become subject to futility, and groans and labors together in pain. The same creation that declares the existence of God, and advertises His glory, also proclaims that He is the Enemy of sin and the Avenger of the crimes of men . . . . But above all, the wrath of God was revealed from heaven when the Son of God came down to manifest the Divine character, and

334 (Hell is real) Matt 5:22, 10:28, 13:41-42, 18:8, 25:46; Rev 19:20, 20:10, 14-15; 2 Thess 1:8-10; Luke 16:23-24; 2 Pet 2:4
335 (Man driven out of the garden) Gen 3:24
336 (The Flood) Gen 7
337 (Destruction of Sodom and Gomorrah) Gen 19:1-29
338 (God's wrath in death) Ezek 3:19; Is 66:16; Heb 9:27; Jude 1:7; Gen 3:19; Rom 5:12, 6:23; 1 Cor 15:26, 55-57
339 (God's wrath in the law) Rom 6:23, 7:9-13; James 1:15, 2:9-11; Gal 3:10; Matt 5:17-45; 1 Cor 15:55-57; 2 Cor 3:7-14
340 (God's wrath toward sin) Lev 17:11, 14; Heb 9:11-18, 22, 13:12; Rev 1:5; Rom 6:23; Ps 145:20; Ezek 18:20; James 1:15; Gal 6:7

when that wrath was displayed in His sufferings and death, in a manner more awful than any of the other evidences God had given before of His hatred of sin. [341]

What's more, the future and eternal punishment of the wicked is now declared in terms more solemn and explicit than before. Under the new dispensation, two revelations are given from heaven, one of wrath, the other of grace. [342]

↑↓3

FOUR REASONS TO MEDITATE ON GOD'S WRATH

As difficult a subject as it is, it is very valuable to meditate on God's wrath. Here are four reasons to start.

First, we tend to minimize sin, to treat it lightly, to gloss over its ugliness, and to make excuses for it. But the more we study and consider God's unqualified hatred of sin and His terrifying vengeance upon it, the more likely are we to realize its seriousness.

Second, contemplating God's wrath should engender a true fear in our souls for God, which may lead to greater reverence for His awesome majesty.

> *"Thus let us offer to God acceptable worship, with reverence and awe, for our God is a consuming fire."* [343]

---

341 (God's wrath on sin at the cross) Prov 6:16-19; Ps 5:4 45:6; Amos 6:8; Heb 1:8
342 (God's wrath and grace) 2 Corinthians 9:8, 12:8-9; 1 Pet 3:18, 5:10; James 4:6; Eph 2:7; Rom 3:24, 5:8; John 3:16; 1 John 4:10 Pink, A.W. *Attributes of God.* n.p, 1930. Print.
343 (God is deserving of worship) Heb 12:28-29; Heb 13:15; 1 Pet 2:5; Rev 5:13, 7:9-17

Third, thinking long and hard on God's wrath in the Scriptures should motivate us to joyful praise of Jesus Christ for having delivered believers heavenward.

> *"To wait for His Son from heaven, whom He raised from the dead, Jesus who delivers us from the wrath to come."* [344]

Fourth, our eagerness or our hesitancy to meditate on God's wrath may be a reliable test of how much we love God. If we do not love God as He truly is, but rather love Him for whom we want Him to be, then can we say we truly love Him? If we love a god without wrath, then do we love a god made in our own image—an idol?

> *"You thought that I was one like yourself."* [345]

↑↓4

If only we stop to think how God's goodness is abused by the majority of mankind, we will come to the same conclusion as William Gurnall, a seventeenth century English clergyman, who said:

> The greatest miracle in the world is God's patience and bounty to an ungrateful world. If a prince has an enemy enter one of his towns, he does not send provisions in to them, but blockades the place and does what he can to starve them out. But the great God, who could destroy every last one of His enemies with a wink, bears with them, and provides for them

---

344 (God is deserving of worship) 1 Thess 1:10; Ps 145:3; Deut 32:3; 1 Pet 2:9; 1 Chron 16:8

345 (Only God is to be worshipped) Ps 50:2; Ex 20:4-5, 34:14; Deut 6:13-14; Ps 63:6-8, 69:32, 81:9; Matt 4:9-10; Php 2:9-11; Rev 4:10-11

161

daily. He can legitimately command us to bless those who curse us, as He Himself does good to the evil and ungrateful constantly! [346] But sinners should never dare to think that they will escape judgment forever; [347] God's mill grinds slowly, but it grinds exceedingly fine. His patience and generosity are glorious and impressive now, but when we see how His goodness is abused and taken for granted, His fury will be all the more terrible and unbearable. There is nothing smoother than the sea when it is still, but when stirred up into a storm, nothing rages stronger. There is nothing as sweet as the patience and goodness of God, [348] but nothing as terrible as His wrath when it takes fire. [349]

↑↓5

SUMMARY

In this chapter, we studied how God's wrath is perfect. It is just. We should not overlook it or try to ignore it because it is an uncomfortable topic. The wrath of God is His eternal contempt for all unrighteousness. If He didn't have wrath against sin, it would be out of character. Sin must be punished, and His wrath is the vehicle. His wrath is part of His perfection. We also studied the four reasons to meditate on His wrath—to take sin more seriously, to encourage a healthy fear of God, to engender grateful-

346 (God is good to sinners) Matt 5:44-45; Rom 2:4, 12:14; 1 Pet 3:9; 2 Pet 3:9; 1 John 4:7-11; Rom 2:4; Ps 34:8, 84:11, 145:9; Heb 9:11; Ps 145:9; Luke 6:34-35; Acts 14:17

347 (God's goodness should not be presumed upon) Matt 3:7; 1 Thess 1:10; Deut 4:9; Is 51:12-13, 65:11-12; Ps 78:11; Acts 24:25; John 5:29; Rev 20:11-13

348 (God's patience) Rom 2:4; Ps 34:8, 84:11, 145:9; Heb 9:11; 2 Peter 3:9

349 Pink, A.W. *Attributes of God*. n.p, 1930. Print.

ness in our hearts to Christ for his salvation from God's wrath, and to know truly in our hearts whether we are worshipping *all* aspects of God, including His wrath. Because we are in Christ, the wrath of God should encourage humility and gratitude in our hearts, not fear. Jesus has cleared the way to God for us sinners, and redeemed us from the wrath of God forever. Hallelujah!

CONTEMPLATIONS

↑↓1

Father, help me list my misconceptions of Your wrath. By Your grace, reveal to me where I am incorrect and how I may know You more clearly. Bring to my memory when I last spoke with someone about Your wrath and how I approached the topic. Draw me through that memory so that I may identify areas You would have me grow in my knowledge of You.

↑↓2

Why have You, God, ordained that You would exercise wrath against people and fallen angels? How is my petty and vindictive wrath different than Yours? How is Your wrath good and mine bad?

↑↓3

Why would Your character be diminished and less glorious if You had no wrath? Why do You thoroughly crush sin in some situations (like the Noahic flood and Sodom and Gomorrah) but not in other situations? How should I ponder the revelation of heaven alongside the revelation of hell?

Give me grace, oh Lord, to ponder wrath. Let my word searches in the Bible point me to many of Your thoughts on Your wrath. Help me see all the ways Your wrath is accomplished in the past, the present, and in Your well-planned future of creation.

↑↓4

How do I minimize sin and treat it too lightly? Just how severe, to what level of intensity, does Your wrath, Lord, punish sin? How should I praise You in Your wrath, when I think of people who are my enemies, whom I don't love as much as I should and who are not saved by You?

Part of me goes to the Psalms of David, praying that You wipe someone out and part of me goes to Your admonishing me to love my neighbor. How do I work through this, Father? Teach me. I am by no means as clear as I should be on this area.

Like Jesus asking Peter whether Peter loved Him, I wonder about myself and how clearly I love You. Reveal to me now, Lord, how I am loving You incorrectly.

↑↓5

Let me list as many ways as I can think of for how mankind abuses Your goodness.

How would I react, if I were You, in wrathfully dealing with those who abuse me and my "goodness?"

Why do You, Lord, command me to love everyone, but You have reserved Your wrath for so many?

Oh my, how different You are, Lord, from me. So infinitely patient. So terrifyingly punishing. I want to make a quippy, light-hearted comment, to ease the tension I feel. Why is this? Why do I want to make light of the difference between us?

Chapter 13

AMAZING GRACE

"Wretched man that I am! Who will set me free from the body of this death? Thanks be to God through Jesus Christ our Lord!"

Romans 7:24-25

Amazing grace! (how sweet the sound)
That saved a wretch like me!
I once was lost, but now am found,
Was blind, but now I see.
'Twas grace that taught my heart to fear,
And grace my fears relieved;
How precious did that grace appear
The hour I first believed! [350]

GOD'S GRACE

God's grace has been defined as "the eternal and absolute free favor of God, manifested in the granting of spiritual and eter-

[350] "Amazing Grace," John Newton, 1779

nal blessings to the guilty and the unworthy." [351] God saves wretched sinners, [352] gives the gift of faith to those who are otherwise incapable of faith [353] and makes the blind see and love the glory of God. [354] And amazingly, God gives His grace to those who completely deserve His eternal wrath in hell. [355]

GOD'S GRACIOUS CHOICE

God's grace is only given to those whom He has chosen to receive it. God sovereignly controls and exclusively bestows His grace only upon whom He pleases: "that grace might reign." [356] If grace "reigns," then it is on the throne, and the occupant of the throne is sovereign.

The Lord declares, "I will be gracious to whom I will be gracious." [357] If God showed grace to all of sinful humanity, people could assume that He was righteously compelled to take them to heaven for having allowed the human race to fall into sin. But God Almighty is under no obligation to any of His creatures, [358] least of all to those who are rebels against Him. [359]

351 Booth, Abraham. *The Reign of Grace: From Its Rise to Its Consummation.* Grand Rapids, MI: Eerdmans, 1949. Print.
352 (God saves sinners) Matt 1:21, 20:28; Gal 1:3-4; 1 Tim 1:15; Tit 2:14; Luke 2:11; Acts 4:12, 5:31, 13:23, 38; Rom 4:25; 1 Cor 15:3
353 (Faith is a gift) Eph 2:8-9; 2 Pet 1:1; Php 1:29; Acts 3:16; 2 Cor 3:5; John 1:12, 4:10, 7:38; Rom 4:16; 2 Tim 1:9; Tit 3:5
354 (God overcomes spiritual blindness) Matt 11:25-27, 13:11, 16:17; 1 Cor 2:14; Eph 1:17-18; Rom 8:7; Heb 10:32; Rev 3:17-18; Acts 26:18; Isa 35:5, 42:7
355 (Sinners deserve eternal punishment) Rev 20:15, 21:8; Matt 13:42, 50, 25:41; Rom 2:6-8; 2 Thess 1:9; 1 Cor 6:9-10; Gal 5:19-21; Eph 5:5
356 (Grace given by God's choice) Rom 5:21
357 (Grace given is a gift of God) Ex 33:19; John 1:14, 17; Deut 9:4-5; 1 Cor 1:29-31; Heb 4:16; Tit 3:5; Eph 2:4; 1 Pet 1:3; Rom 4:2, 9:15-18, 11:6
358 (God not obligated to creatures) Ps 115:3, 135:6; Matt 20:15; Deut 7:6-7, 14:2, 26:19, 28:9; Rom 11:4-6; Dan 4:35; Ex 19:6
359 (All have sinned against God) Prov 20:9; Rom 3:9-12, 23; James 3:2; Job 15:14-16; 1 Kin 8:46; Eccl 7:20; 1 John 1:8, 10; Jer 2:35

↑↓1

God's grace is also eternal, predestined by God in eternity past when He decreed everything that should come to pass. [360] God has never been caught off-guard nor been surprised, and His grace is not an alternative "Plan B" in response to human sin. Grace was planned before it was exercised; God determined who would receive it and why before it was given to them.

> "Who saved us and called us to a holy calling, not because of our works, but because of His own purpose and grace, which He gave us in Christ Jesus before the ages began." [361]

↑↓2

God's grace is freely given as a gift, with no expectation of repayment. God's grace cannot be bought, earned, nor won. If it could be, it would no longer be grace. [362] The absolutely perfect and pure favor of God cannot be combined with any conception of human merit any more than oil and water can be combined and become one substance. [363] This is because people are so wretched in and of themselves, so spiritually blind and sinful to their core, that there is no way for them to come into relationship with a pure and holy God. [364]

---

360 (God decrees all things) Ps 139:16; Acts 2:23, 3:18, 4:28, 26:22-23; Eph 1:4; Luke 22:22, 24:26-27; Heb 2:10

361 (God saves us apart from works) 2 Tim 1:9; Gal 2:16; Rom 3:20, 27-28, 4:2; Tit 3:5; 1 Cor 1:29-31; Eph 2:9; Acts 13:39

362 (Grace is freely given) Rom 3:24, 27, 4:3-5, 11:6; Tit 2:11, 3:7; Deut 9:4-5; Eph 2:4; 1 Pet 1:3

363 (We can't earn grace) Rom 3:20, 28, 4:4-5; Gal 2:16, 3:2, 5, 14; Ps 143:2; Heb 6:4

364 (Depravity of every man) Rom 5:12; Eph 2:1-3; 1 Kings 8:46; Ps 130:3; 1 Cor 15:22; Prov 20:9; Eccl 7:20; Rom 3:23; James 3:2

↑↓3

EXAMINING OUR HEARTS

Does it trouble, irritate, and perhaps even anger you that God's divine grace is eternal, free, and sovereign? Is it painfully humbling that God should have formed His plan of salvation in eternity past without even consulting His creatures? Is it downright insulting that grace cannot be earned or won by any of our efforts? The truth that God graciously discriminates and calls out certain sinners but not others can provoke heated and noisy protests from people who demand that everything be "fair." [365]

On the other hand, are you irresistibly drawn to God's gracious choice of helpless sinners? [366] Are you sobered as you realize that all people since Adam and Eve have been incapable of saving themselves from God's wrath? [367] Do you feel a sense of helplessness, perhaps despair, and the need for a savior as you ponder the reality that even the tiniest speck of sin keeps one from fellowship with the Lord God of the universe? [368]

> *"Wretched man that I am! Who will set me free from the body of this death? Thanks be to God through Jesus Christ our Lord!"* [369]

---

365 (God has a chosen people) Deut 7:7, 10:14-15; Ps 33:12; Col 3:12; 1 Thess 5:9; Rev 17:14; Rom 1:6, 8:33; Luke 18:7
366 (Grace draws us) 2 Tim 2:25-26; Php 1:29; Acts 16:14; Luke 24:45; Ps 119:18; 1 John 5:20; Job 36:10, 15; John 6:44; Hosea 11:4
367 (We can't save ourselves) Jer 13:23; Job 14:4; John 6:44, 65; 1 Cor 2:14, 4:7; Matt 7:16-18, 12:33; 2 Cor 3:5
368 (We need a savior) Mark 2:17; Luke 15:4, 19:10; Tit 3:3-7; 1 Cor 6:9-11; Ezek 34:11, 16; Matt 9:13, 15:24
369 (Jesus Christ is the Savior) Rom 7:24-25; Tit 2:14; 1 Tim 1:15, 2 Tim 4:18; Heb 9:14; Matt 1:21; Luke 19:10; 2 Cor 5:21; Gal 1:3-4

Examine your heart and think through God's grace. Perhaps you have been harboring some deeper-seated animosity toward God. Maybe you have been so self-righteous, self-centered, and self-reliant that you have not recognized your inner rebellion toward the one Almighty God of the universe. [370] If so, ask God in His grace to draw you close to Him, to help you understand His grace fully. Ask God to reveal the glorious beauty of the gospel, the good news of His grace.

↑↓4

THE FIGUREHEAD AND STANDARD BEARER OF ALL GRACE

The grace of God comes to us through the Lord Jesus Christ. "The law was given by Moses, grace and truth came by Jesus Christ." [371] This does not mean that God never exercised grace toward anyone before Christ. [372] But grace and truth were fully revealed and perfectly exemplified when the Redeemer, Jesus Christ, came to earth and died for His people upon the cross. Christ the Mediator is the ultimate standard of God's grace, and it is through Him alone that grace flows. [373]

> *"Much more have the grace of God, and the free gift by the grace of that one man, Jesus Christ abounded. . . much more will those who receive the abundance of grace, and of the free gift of righteousness reign in life by the one man Jesus Christ . . .so that*

---

370 (Depravity of man) John 8:34, 44; Eph 2:1-2, 4:17-19; Tit 3:3; Eccl 9:3; Gen 6:5, 8:21; Jer 17:9; Mark 7:21-23; John 3:19

371 (Grace is from Jesus Christ) John 1:17; Rom 3:20-24, 5:21; 2 Cor 12:8-9; Acts 6:8, 15:11; Eph 2:8-9, 4:7; Heb 4:16; 1 Pet 4:10; 2 Pet 1:2; James 4:6; Tit 2:11

372 (God shows grace even before Jesus came) Gen 6:8, 19:19; Ex 22:27, 33:19, 34:5-7; Ps 31:19, 84:11; Jer 31:2, 14

373 (Grace comes through Jesus Christ) John 1:14; Rom 3:20-24, 5:20-21; Eph 4:7; 2 Cor 12:8-9; Acts 6:8, 15:11; 1 Pet 4:10; 2 Pet 1:2; Tit 2:11

grace . . . might reign through righteousness leading to eternal life through Jesus Christ our Lord." [374]

The grace of God is proclaimed in the gospel, [375] and that gospel is to the self-righteous Jew a "stumbling block," and to the conceited and philosophizing Greek "foolishness." [376] Why? Because there is nothing at all in it that will accommodate human pride.

The grace of God should humble us and utterly destroy all our notions of our own goodness and our ideas that we deserve heaven. Apart from Christ and His gracious saving work on the cross, all of life is hopeless. The gospel addresses men as guilty, condemned, perishing criminals. The gospel declares that, unless we are saved by grace, we cannot be saved at all.

"And you were dead in your trespasses and sins, in which you formerly walked according to the course of this world, according to the prince of the power of the air, of the spirit that is now working in the sons of disobedience. Among them we too all formerly lived in the lusts of our flesh, indulging the desires of the flesh and of the mind, and were by nature children of wrath, even as the rest. But God, being rich in mercy, because of His great love with which He loved us, even when we were dead in our transgressions, made us alive together with Christ (by grace you have been saved), and raised us up with Him, and seated us with Him in the Heavenly places in Christ Jesus, so that in the ages to come He might show the surpassing riches of His grace in kindness toward us in Christ Jesus. For by grace you have been saved

---

374 (Grace, a free gift from Jesus Christ) Rom 5:15, 17, 21; Rom 3:20-24; 2 Cor 12:8-9; Acts 6:8, 15:11; Eph 2:8-9, 4:7; 2 Pet 1:2; Heb 4:16

375 (Grace proclaimed in the gospel) Acts 11:23, 13:43, 20:24, 32; Rom 5:13; 1 Tim 1:14; 2 Cor 6:1; Eph 3:2, 7; Col 1:6

376 (Gospel is foolishness) 1 Cor 1:18, 21, 23-25; 1 Cor 2:14; 2 Cor 4:3; 2 Thess 2:10

through faith; and that not of yourselves, it is the gift of God; not as a result of works, so that no one may boast. For we are His workmanship, created in Christ Jesus for good works, which God prepared beforehand so that we would walk in them." [377]

↑↓5

SUMMARY

In this chapter, we saw how God's grace is granted to those who are totally deserving of spending eternity in hell. God chooses who receives and who does not receive His grace. And lastly, we meditated on the fact that grace and truth were fully revealed and perfectly exemplified when God the Redeemer, Jesus Christ, came to earth and died for His people upon the cross. Christ the Mediator is the ultimate standard of God's grace and it is through Him alone that grace flows.

CONTEMPLATIONS

↑↓1

Lord, do I misapply, perhaps overextend the word "grace?" Teach me in Your Word how Your sovereign grace is different than Your mercy, Your general goodness and "graciousness" to people. Is it really just a misunderstanding, or do I and others lump sovereign grace into Your niceness for other good and bad reasons?

Am I too democratic in my thinking since I have never lived under a human king? Let me contemplate the differences in living in a democracy versus a kingdom and how that can affect my relationship with You. Let me also see how that affects others' opinions on

377 (God's gift to sinners) Eph 2:1-9

the truth of Your sovereign grace in salvation.

Teach me how I may share Your grace with others, both Christians and non-Christians, in a way that lifts up Your clear sovereignty over sinners yet also draws them to appreciate You. Let me think of those times when I've shared Your sovereign grace with others and how they did not want to recognize You as being so strong, so high and mighty to save.

↑↓2

The more I ponder Your decrees in eternity past, the more so many Scriptures begin tying logically together. I love You for knowing all, and it makes good sense that You do since You planned it all at once in eternity past. Draw me into my ponderings of Your grace and Your massive and perfect plan for everything You created. Let me worship You in truth and glory!

Why did You plan everything like You did? The bottom line answer to every "Why?" question of life always ends up leading to Your glory. Yet perhaps I am using the phrase "It's all to glorify God" a bit too easily, like a trite cliché. Am I? If I am, please forgive me. Also, show me Thy glory more deeply as I ponder Your grace in Your plan, established long, long ago.

↑↓3

Yes, of course I've heard that Your grace is a gift. But do I in many ways still try to earn my salvation? Or do I seek to repay You for Your gift? If I do, help me to see how I act this way in my life. Reveal what I am ignorant of that I might not cheapen Your grace.

For some reason, I think of the analogy of a person in a boating accident, drowning, waving his arms, asking for help, and You throw him a line and lifebuoy and "pull him in." But Your grace is even bigger than that because the person drowning is really unconscious and drowning, not even moving to ask You to save him. Wow . . . that's a gift. Let me ponder our depravity and ignorance of You prior to being rescued.

↑↓4

So many emotions are possible when we think of Your grace. Guide me to think on Your grace and the many emotions that surround it. Help me understand these emotions and why they occur.

↑↓5

The gospel. Your gospel. Wow! Dozens of angles seem to exist to approach Your gospel of grace right now. Help me to write out those angles of understanding that I might praise You for the good news of Jesus Christ.

Have I skipped over Your law too quickly as I've embraced the gospel and Your saving power in my life? Show me afresh how I should ponder Your law and how it relates to me today and how it perhaps amplifies Your grace. Should I be living differently in light of the gospel, Your grace, and Your law? If I am missing some parts to a more full life in You, please show me.

Chapter 14

LORD, HAVE MERCY

"Come to me, all who labor and are heavy laden,
and I will give you rest. Take my yoke upon you, and learn from
me, for I am gentle and lowly in heart, and you will find rest for
your souls. For my yoke is easy, and my burden is light."

Matthew 11:28-30

GOD'S BLANKET OF MERCY OVER ALL CREATION
Mercy is God's compassion and goodness toward those who are in
misery and suffering. Whenever God demonstrates compassion or
relieves people from their calamity or agony, we are witnessing the
beautiful mercy of God. Our need for mercy began at the fall when
calamity and distress came upon creation.

↑↓1

All of fallen creation experiences mercy whenever God showers
down any good gift from above. Animals and plants, as well as the

rest of creation, still exhibit some degree of God's glory, [378] and in His mercy, the Lord sustains them all. He still sends sunshine to the world, and gives everything a season to flourish.

"The LORD is good to all, and His mercy is over all that He has made." [379] Nevertheless, even though all creation experiences God's mercy, it is still only ever given as He sees fit. God is not required to show mercy to anyone, but it pleases Him to have mercy on some and pass over others. Those who receive mercy do so because of God's pleasure to demonstrate His goodness. If God's mercy were rooted in the simple need for mercy, then God would have mercy on everyone. God's choice to show mercy is not influenced or grounded in our need for it.

"I will have mercy on whom I have mercy, and I will have compassion on whom I have compassion." [380]

In general, people may be quick to affirm the mercy of God. However, this affirmation can lead to presuming on God's mercy, rather than trusting it. We should never believe that God's mercy will mean that He will overlook sin or compromise justice.

↑↓2

Our need for this mercy is great, and let us take care not to presume upon it. Jesus spoke of a rich man who was in torment in Hades. [381]

---

378 (Earth is filled with His glory) Isa 6:3; Num 14:21; Ps 72:19, 96:7-9, 139:7-12; Hab 2:14; 1 Kings 8:27; 2 Chr 6:18; Jer 23:23-24; Rev 5:13

379 (God shows a degree of mercy to all) Ps 145:9; Ps 147:8, 18; Matt 5:45; Acts 14:17; Job 5:10; Luke 6:35; James 1:5; Prov 25:21-22; Rom 12:20-21

380 (God has mercy on whom He wills) Ex 33:19; Rom 9:15-16, 25-26; Eph 2:4-5, 7; Tit 3:3-5; 1 Pet 2:9-10; Hosea 1:6, 9-10, 2:23

381 (Rich man in Hades desired mercy) Luke 16:19-31

The rich man was in anguish and pleaded with Abraham for just a drop of water to cool his tongue. He wanted relief from his agony; he really wanted mercy!

God's mercy and the goodness from which it springs does not negate His justice. On the contrary, God's strong demand for justice amplifies our need for His mercy! Nobody should ever say to himself that God would never send him to hell because He's too merciful. Take careful note of Scripture when it says that God *"will by no means clear the guilty."* [382]

God's mercy is a missive blessing and a profound reminder of His goodness. *"O give thanks unto the LORD; for He is good: for His mercy endureth forever."* [383] God's mercy is so great that praising Him for such an awesome gift should be a tremendous joy, yet we know that not everyone praises God and loves Him and His mercy.

↑↓3

When a wicked farmer who cares nothing about God receives refreshing rain on his crop, he is experiencing mercy. When a corrupt businessman receives a newborn child from the hand of God, he is experiencing God's mercy. When the famished and thirsty receive food and water, this too is God's precious mercy.

THE END OF GOD'S MERCY

Mercy expressed in this way, to those who aren't Christians, is limit-

382 (God will not compromise justice) Ps 2:12, 9:17; Luke 13:3; Rom 8:3; Deut 29:18-20; Ex 23:31, 34:7; Josh 24:19; Job 10:14; Nah 1:3
383 (God's mercy endures forever) Ps 136:1, KJV; 1 Chr 15:41, 16:34, KJV; 2 Chr 5:13, 7:3, 6, 20:21 KJV; Ezra 3:11, KJV; Jer 33:11, KJV

ed, temporary, and short-lived. It lasts only the duration of this present life. Mercy does not extend to them beyond the grave. The mercy that once held back the wrath of God will be released so that wrath will be poured out, without mercy.

When people who want nothing to do with God draw their last breath in this life, they will no longer experience God's mercy. God's mercy will be foreign to them, and it will be forever out of reach. As Scripture says:

> *"For this is a people without discernment; therefore He who made them will not have compassion on them; He who formed them will show them no favor."* [384]

It Is Merciful That God Is Just

Even God's own judgment is an act of mercy toward those who are redeemed by Jesus Christ. If sin and wickedness were allowed to continue, the children of God would have to endure the persecution, blasphemy, and other wickedness in their midst. However, God has promised that He will relieve His children of distress from the wicked. [385] What a comfort it should be to the children of God to know that God will deal with terrorism groups, genocide, rapists, murderers, liars, thieves, and anyone else who grieves those who are His!

> "After this I heard what seemed to be the loud voice of a great multitude in heaven, crying out, 'Hallelujah! Salvation and glory and power belong to our God, for His judgments are true and just; for He has judged the great prostitute who corrupt-

384 (God will judge) Isa 27:11; Ezek 5:11, 7:4, 9, 8:18, 9:5,10, 24:14; Jer 21:7; 2 Thess 1:8-9

385 (God will have mercy on His children) Ps 86:5, 136:15; Eph 2:4; Tit 3:5; Heb 4:16; 1 Pet 1:3; Rev 21:27, 22:14-15

ed the earth with her immorality, and has avenged on her the blood of His servants.' Once more they cried out, 'Hallelujah! The smoke from her goes up forever and ever.'" [386]

Ever since the fall, all mankind has experienced suffering, frustrations, alienation, and misery. People often turn to drugs, alcohol, pornography, and other forms of relief from these pains. None of these actually relieve the suffering, but instead, they often multiply the problem. Only the mercy of God provides true relief.

> *"Come to me, all who labor and are heavy laden, and I will give you rest. Take my yoke upon you, and learn from me, for I am gentle and lowly in heart, and you will find rest for your souls. For my yoke is easy, and my burden is light."* [387]

↑↓4

THE LORD'S MERCY TOWARD HIS CHILDREN IS ABUNDANT

God has a special mercy for Christians. [388] He sacrificed His Son on the cross to demonstrate that He does not compromise His justice in order to provide His eternal mercy toward us. The Lord has abundant mercy, [389] and Scripture invites us to approach the throne of grace *"that we may receive mercy and find grace to help in time*

---

386 (God will punish those who grieve His children) Rev 19:1-3; Rev 6:9-11; Gen 12:3, 27:29; Num 24:9; Rom 2:2; Matt 12:41; Heb 11:7; Jer 3:11; Ezek 16:51-52; Ps 54:5, 143:12

387 (God invites all who need mercy) Matt 11:28-30; John 6:37, 7:37, 10:28, 17:12; Ezek 33:11; Luke 13:34; Matt 23:37

388 (God has special mercy for Christians) Matt 9:27, 15:22; 1 Pet 1:3; Ps 51:1, 86:5; 1 John 2:25, 5:11; 2 Thess 3:3; Jude 1:24; John 17:12

389 (God has abundant mercy) 1 Pet 1:3; 2 Cor 1:3; Eph 3:20; Num 14:18; Ps 86:8, 15; Tit 3:5; 2 Cor 9:8; Ex 34:6-7; Neh 9:17; Jon 4:2

of need." [390] May His children be encouraged and comforted by the Comforter Himself with unfailing mercy!

SUMMARY

God's mercy is a reflection of His deep love and goodness, and He shows His mercy to all creation. He demonstrates compassion and relieves people from their calamity or agony. If a wicked farmer who cares nothing about God receives the refreshing rain on his crop or a corrupt businessman receives a newborn child from the hand of God, he is experiencing God's mercy. However, God's mercy does not extend beyond the grave. Sin and wickedness must be punished. And in the ultimate act of mercy, God sacrificed His own son for our sins so we could live with Him in heaven forever.

CONTEMPLATIONS

↑↓1

Lord, have I been harsh and judgmental toward those to whom You are showing mercy, those whom I may feel are undeserving? Let me recognize my own sin, that I deserve mercy no more than they, and help me to pray for them in love instead of judgment.

↑↓2

Bring to my memory when I last spoke with someone about Your mercy and how I approached the topic. Draw me through that

390 (God invites us to receive mercy) Heb 4:16; Heb 7:19, 25, 10:19; Eph 2:18, 3:12; John 10:9; Rom 5:2; James 4:8; Zech 1:3

memory so that I may identify areas in which You would grow my knowledge of You.

↑↓3

Give me grace, oh Lord, to ponder mercy. Let my word searches in the Bible point me to many of Your thoughts on Your mercy. Help me see all the ways Your mercy is accomplished, in the past, in the present, and in Your well-planned future of creation.

↑↓4

How should I praise You in Your mercy when I think of people who are my enemies, whom I don't love as much as I should and who are not saved by You? Part of me goes to the Psalms of David, praying that You wipe someone out, and part of me goes to Your admonishing me to love my neighbor. How do I work through this, Father? Teach me. I am by no means as clear as I should be on this area.

Chapter 15

UNIQUELY PATIENT

"The Lord is slow to anger and abounding in steadfast love,
forgiving iniquity and transgression, but He will by no means clear
the guilty, visiting the iniquity of the fathers on the children,
to the third and the fourth generation."

Numbers 14:18

GOD'S PATIENCE FLOWS FROM HIS KINDNESS

Impatience makes it difficult to tolerate any other length of time than "Now!" The world is full of people who have agendas and the desire to accomplish them as quickly as possible. Our modern accommodations thrive on the impatience of the consumer. However, standing in contrast to the way mankind lives is God's awesome patience and steadfast love!

> *"But You, O Lord, are a God merciful and gracious, slow to*
> *anger and abounding in steadfast love and faithfulness."* [391]

---

391 (God is patient) Ps 86:15; Ps 103:8; 2 Pet 3:9, 15; Num 14:18; Ex 34:6; Joel 2:13; Isa 7:13; Rom 2:4, 9:22-24

God's patience comes from His infinite goodness. [392] While we may not see the word "patience" frequently in Scripture, we can be sure to find God's expression of it on every page. God's patience reveals His willingness to work with creation over a period of time, rather than demand an instantaneous result. God's patience is of great value to us because without it we wouldn't enjoy His other blessings.

We benefit from God's patience whenever we sin and, instead of experiencing the immediate thunderous clap of His righteous judgment, we draw a breath of undeserved air. This priceless moment of kindness and mercy coming from the patience of the Lord is cause for praise!

> *"For my name's sake I defer my anger, for the sake of my praise I restrain it for you, that I may not cut you off."* [393]

↑↓1

GOD'S PATIENCE HOLDS BACK HIS WRATH UPON THE WICKED

Mankind has a history of offending God and rebelling against Him, [394] but that behavior is not always met with immediate and swift response. [395] This expression of God's patience is rooted tenderly in self-control. God is not controlled by anything and, therefore, never acts impulsively or becomes overwhelmed by emotions like

---

392 (Patience comes from God's goodness) Ex 34:6; Neh 9:16-17; Jon 4:2; Rom 2:4; Ps 86:5

393 (God's patience is cause for praise) Isa 48:9

394 (Man's rebellion against God) Deut 9:23; Ps 107:11; Ezek 20:8; Isa 53:6, 59:12-13, 64:6; Dan 9:5; Rom 3:23; Eccl 7:20, 29

395 (God is patient with sinners) Num 14:18; Neh 9:30; Isa 53:7; 1 Pet 2:23, 3:9, 20; Luke 13:8; Acts 13:18; Jer 11:19; Heb 12:3; Rev 2:3

fallen people do. [396] God is aware of every sin on earth and is angry with the wicked every day, yet He holds back the fullness of His wrath because of His patience.

> *"What if God, desiring to show His wrath and to make known His power, has endured with much patience vessels of wrath prepared for destruction?"* [397]

How many of us could endure the constant rebellion that God experiences from all of mankind and still be considered patient? Remember, only one sin is necessary for God's unbridled wrath without mercy. [398] Yet all of history is filled with unmentionable atrocities and demonstrations of the patience of the Lord.

> *"The Lord is slow to anger and abounding in steadfast love, forgiving iniquity and transgression, but He will by no means clear the guilty, visiting the iniquity of the fathers on the children, to the third and the fourth generation."* [399]

God's patience reveals amazing self-control, and should not be interpreted as indifference, laziness, passiveness, or ignorance toward wickedness. What is so heavily presumed upon by sinners should move those who recognize the patience of God to adoration of and gratitude for the Lord's self-control. When we realize how much our sin deserves punishment, we can begin to comprehend the long-suffering and patience of our Lord.

---

396 (Self-control and godliness) Tit 1:8, 2:12; 1 Cor 4:12-13, 9:25; Gal 5:23; 1 Pet 1:13, 5:8; 2 Pet 1:5-9; 1 Thess 4:3-7; Prov 29:11

397 (God holds back wrath because of patience) Rom 9:22; Num 14:18; Ex 34:6; Neh 9:16-17; Ps 145:8; Joel 2:13; Jon 4:2; Nah 1:3; Isa 43:24

398 (Sin deserves the wrath of God) James 2:10; Rom 1:18, 2:5-6; Nah 1:2; Rev 19:15; Isa 13:11, 26:21; Ps 99:8; Amos 3:14; 1 Thess 4:6; Prov 11:21

399 (God is patient with sinners) Num 14:18

↑↓2

GOD'S PATIENCE IS A REFUGE BUT NOT AN OPPORTUNITY

The Lord's patience is a place of refuge for sinners. When we witness just how much and how long the Lord endures with sinful people, we can rest in His patience as though it were a strong fortress. It is a comfort and a delight to know that the Lord isn't in heaven with a watchful eye ready to dash us to pieces, but instead, He is willing to bear with us and show kindness and patience toward all who turn to Him. [400]

But presumption on His patience is no refuge at all and instead is a snare. Untold numbers of people presume upon God's patience and believe they are getting away with sin. This presumption is not a comfort or a delight; rather it hardens the heart and perpetuates sin and rebellion against God.

> *"These things you have done, and I have been silent; you thought that I was one like yourself. But now I rebuke you and lay the charge before you."* [401]

The wickedness of man views the patience of God as an opportunity to exploit His goodness. But the foolishness of that inclination of the heart is readily obvious, as God knows what is in man. We should not see God's patience as an occasion for sin but repentance!

> *"Or do you presume on the riches of His kindness and forbearance and patience, not knowing that God's kindness is meant to*

---

400 (God is slow to anger) Ps 86:5, 15, 103:3, 130:4, 145:8; Joel 2:13; Rom 15:5; Mic 7:18; Ex 34:6; Jon 4:2; Dan 9:9

401 (God's patience is not to be presumed upon) Ps 50:21; Ps 90:8; Eccl 8:11; Isa 51:12-13, 57:11; 2 Kin 19:4; Ezek 24:14; Num 23:19; Neh 9:17

lead you to repentance?" [402]

"The Lord is not slow in keeping His promise, as some under-stand slowness. Instead He is patient with you, not wanting anyone to perish, but everyone to come to repentance." [403]

↑↓3

BELIEVERS BENEFIT IMMEASURABLY FROM GOD'S PATIENCE

God's patience should not be seen as merely something people can benefit from, but also a demonstration of who He is. God's patience is an amazing and vivid testimony of who God is, not just something He does. This is a marvelous thing to contemplate. Against the backdrop of God's hostility, anger, and hatred toward sin, we can witness the marvelous patience of the Lord.

God's children experience His patience when He treats them as their loving heavenly Father. *"And we know that for those who love God all things work together for good, for those who are called according to His purpose."* [404] The children of God benefit immeasurably from His patience. But the children of God are not to be mere recipients of God's patience; they are also to imitate it!

THE FRUIT OF PATIENCE SHOULD BE EVIDENT IN BELIEVERS AS WELL

Fruit produces after its own kind, and if the children of God are truly His, they will demonstrate patience, the fourth fruit of the

---

402 (God's patience leads to repentance) Rom 2:4; Isa 30:18; Luke 18:7; James 5:7
403 (God is patient toward the called) 2 Pet 3:9; 2 Pet 3:15; Rev 2:21
404 (God's patience benefits Christians) Rom 8:28; Rom 9:24; 1 Cor 1:9, 7:17; Eph 4:1, 4; 2 Tim 1:9; Eccl 8:12; Ps 37:11, 18-19

Spirit. [405] The history of the children of God is filled with people who were patient with the world. Those who follow Christ demonstrate patience as they endure trials, tribulations, and persecutions from the rest of the world. If we are really co-heirs with Christ and children of God, then we should demonstrate a similar kind of patience as He did with His accusers.

It is easy to believe that we need to be patient with each other. But our imitation of patience is not limited to other Christians, or the world. We must also be patient toward the Lord. Impatience with the Lord leads to not trusting in God's wisdom and timing and trusting in something far more fallible—ourselves.

In light of all of these things, Christians should be patient in a world full of impatience. Christians should have confidence in the Lord who has appointed all things to happen at the proper time. This understanding is not limited to our daily affairs, but should extend to the most anticipated event in all of humanity's history— the Lord's soon return!

> *"He who testifies to these things says, 'Surely I am coming soon.' Amen. Come, Lord Jesus! The grace of the Lord Jesus be with all. Amen."* [406]

↑↓4

---

405 (God's children are patient) Gal 5:22-23; Eph 4:2; Col 1:11, 3:12-13; James 1:19; Prov 14:17, 29, 16:32, 19:11; Eccl 7:9
406 (Christians are patient toward God) 1 Cor 13:4; Gen 12:4-7, 18:10-15; John 18:56; Heb 6:15; Rev 22:20-21; Isa 30:18, 40:31; Ps 27:13-14, 130:5-6; Lam 3:25

SUMMARY

God's patience is quiet. It is in the background, and sometimes it's easy to forget that God is quietly being patient with us. As believers, we should be stunned with gratitude when we once again realize the immensity of His patience. It is a beautiful attribute of God.

And as fruit produces from its own kind, so we as believers should also bear the fruit of His patience, by exercising patience ourselves in our everyday lives. We should not view His patience as an opportunity to sin but as an opportunity to be grateful and repent of our sins. We should thank Him every day for this long-suffering endurance of our weakness.

CONTEMPLATIONS

↑↓1

Lord, the fact that You continue to bear with me demonstrates Your goodness. My lack of goodness does not cause You to abandon Your goodness. You are good, and Your lovingkindness endures forever. Your patience with me is a constant reminder of this truth. Thank You for Your goodness. Remind me of all the ways Your patience reveals Your unique character. I love that patience is not just something You do or show, but it is something You are.

↑↓2

Self-control is hard for me to exhibit even when I am barely wronged. Mankind is in constant rebellion, and yet You stay Your hand of judgment. Even as Your anger burns, You control Your response according to Your perfect and sovereign will. As You sanctify me, Lord, teach me to control myself; help me to control my anger and to exhibit even a small measure of Your self-control.

↑↓3

Lord, I know I have presumed upon Your patience way too many times to count. Don't let Your tender mercies harden my heart to sin. I am grateful for how You endure my pitiful ways, but let sin grieve my heart as much as it grieves Yours.

Praise be to You for Your gracious choices—don't let me take those choices for granted and thus provoke You to wrath.

↑↓4

Your patience accomplishes many things for Your purposes, Lord. Your Word specifically says that patience leads us to repentance. You endure my sin so that I can repent. You put up with mankind's obstinacy and rebellion so they may turn to You. What amazing love You show in Your patience. Thank You for so many chances. Thank You for the opportunity to repent. Please continue to bear my wrongs, Lord. But let them be fewer every day. Let Your patience work to bear fruit in my life, the fruit of repentance.

Chapter 16

GREAT IS THY FAITHFULNESS

"O Lord God of hosts, who is mighty as You are, O Lord,
with Your faithfulness all around You?"

Psalm 89:8

Everything About God Is Faithful

We have all experienced both faithfulness and unfaithfulness. Have you ever had someone break a promise he made to you? Have you secretly confided in someone only to find out later that she told someone else your secret?

Have you ever confidently hired someone to do a job, only to find out later that he didn't do it correctly? Sadly, we've all felt the pain and frustration of people breaking promises and spilling secrets we thought they'd keep.

As much as you and I may point our fingers at others, how might we convict ourselves of similar unfaithfulness? In subtle or obvious ways, we have also failed and disappointed people. As humans, we are all awash in a pool of perfidy. Yet this all pales in comparison to our unfaithfulness toward God.

> *"For our fathers have been unfaithful and have done evil in the sight of the LORD our God, and have forsaken Him and turned their faces away from the dwelling place of the LORD, and have turned their backs."* [407]

↑↓1

Regardless of whether we recognize our unfaithfulness, His faithfulness stands in complete contrast to everything else. It is helpful and enlightening to compare our failings to His perfect and glorious faithfulness.

> *"The works of His hands are faithful and just; all His precepts are trustworthy; they are established forever and ever, to be performed with faithfulness and uprightness. He sent redemption to His people; He has commanded His covenant forever. Holy and awesome is His name!"* [408]

His Faithfulness Is Rooted In His Truthfulness

Because of our culture and history of unfaithfulness, sometimes we need convincing of His faithfulness. God knows very well our doubts and provides some comforting words in Scripture to help overcome our lack of faith in Him and

---

407 (Our unfaithfulness) 2 Chr 29:6; Rom 3:3-4, 10:16; 1 Chr 5:25; Deut 4:25-27; Jer 3, 5:6, 19, 7:26; Heb 3:12-19, 4:2; Ex 34:15; Ps 78:17-19, 95:8-11; Isa 50:10, 65:2; Acts 7:51; Neh 1:8; Deut 8:19-20; Judg 10:13
408 (God's Word is faithful) Ps 111:7-9; Ps 19:7, 9, 93:5; Isa 40:8; Matt 5:18, 24:35; Luke 16:17

what He says. He provides these evidences by telling us who He is and also by displaying His acts of faithfulness. [409]

First, faithfulness is essential to who God is. Without it, God would not be God. God considers our appreciation of His faithfulness as a vital part of knowing Him. *"Know therefore that the Lord your God, He is God, the faithful God."* [410] For God to be unfaithful, He would have to act contrary to His nature, which is impossible. *"If we are faithless, He remains faithful, for He cannot deny Himself."* [411] Not only is God faithful, but faithfulness surrounds Him.

> *"O Lord God of hosts, who is like You, O mighty Lord? Your faithfulness also surrounds You."* [412]

It is important to note that God's faithfulness is rooted in His truthfulness. [413] These two attributes are related to each other, as God could not be faithful unless He is also absolutely and most completely truthful. Scripture tells us God cannot lie, and that everything He does is faithful and true. This is so much the case that the Bible even calls Jesus Christ by the name *"Faithful and True."* [414]

We want to avoid the notion that God is only relaying information from a limited perspective. People are truthful only as far as they're able to comprehend the information they're sharing. God is truth-

409 (God's faithfulness) Ps 111:7-9; 2 Thess 3:3, Gen 32:10; Ps 33:4, 36:5, 89:2, 119:90; Isa 25:1; Deut 7:9; 1 Cor 1:0
410 (God is faithful) Deut 7:9; 1 Cor 10:13; 2 Cor 1:18; 1 Thess 5:24; 2 Thess 3:3; Heb 10:23; Isa 49:7; 2 Tim 2:13
411 (God is steadfast) 2 Tim 2:13; Num 23:19; Tit 1:2; Heb 6:18; 1 John 1:9; Ps 143:1; 1 Cor 1:9, 10:13; Deut 7:9
412 (God is surrounded by faithfulness) Ps 89:8
413 (Faithfulness and truthfulness go together) Matt 22:16; Ex 34:6; Ps 25:5, 10, 31:5, 40:11, 57:10, 69:13, 108:4
414 (Jesus is Faithful and True) Rev 19:11

ful in a complete sense because God *"is perfect in knowledge."* [415] Because God has complete knowledge, [416] we can be assured God knows exactly what He is saying to us, and God knows everything necessary to qualify what He says. Without His complete knowledge, we would have reason to question His truthfulness.

↑↓2

GOD'S FAITHFULNESS ENDURES ACROSS ALL TIME

Second, Scripture testifies of God's faithfulness through acts spanning the entire course of history. [417] God promised as long as the earth remained, the seasons *"shall not cease"* and also that never again would there *"be a flood to destroy the earth."* [418] We have over four thousand years of God's faithfulness demonstrated in both of these promises that continue today!

Scripture also records a promise God made to Abraham. Abraham was told his descendants would be enslaved for four hundred years and God would *"judge the nation whom they will serve, and afterward they will come out with many possessions."* [419] The Lord did not forget His promise and brought them out of slavery *"to the very day."* [420] The exactness, the perfection, the certainty of God's words were demonstrated to an entire nation of people!

---

415 (God is perfect in knowledge) Job 37:16; Job 36:4; 1 Sam 2:3; 1 John 3:20
416 (God has complete knowledge) Dan 2:21-22; Ps 90:7-8, 103:13-14, 139:1-6, 147:4; Heb 4:12-13; Matt 10:30; Isa 40:26
417 (God's faithfulness throughout history) Gen 50:20; Gen 41:28-32; I Sam 16:13; 2 Sam 5:4; Luke 2:34; Heb 11
418 (God's faithfulness to His promise to Noah) Gen 8:22, 9:11
419 (God's faithfulness to Abraham) Gen 15:13-14
420 (God's exacting faithfulness) Ex 12:40-41; Gen 15:13; Acts 7:6

Perhaps for the ancient Jewish nation, the most eagerly awaited and talked about event of its day was the anticipated coming of the Messiah. These famous words of Scripture, penned 700 years beforehand, show the beauty of God's faithfulness in the fulfillment of His promise in the birth of Christ.

> *"Therefore the Lord Himself will give you a sign: Behold, a virgin will be with child and bear a son, and she will call His name Immanuel."* [421]

The birth of Christ is a profound demonstration of God's faithfulness, but we are only scratching the surface of God's recorded faithfulness. We may feel that God's promise to Abraham and His prophecy concerning the birth of Christ were amazing. None of that comes close to the promises made concerning Christ's triumph at the cross, [422] made in the Garden of Eden, [423] and even before the foundation of the world. [424]

Even Christ's words on the cross, *"It is finished,"* carry with them His faithfulness. They communicate His faithfulness to the Father, that He accomplished what He was sent to do on the cross, and it reveals His Faithfulness to His people because by it, He accomplished their salvation. Christ was willing to give up everything He had to remain faithful, all the way to His last breath. Scripture points to this very moment as proof of God's faithfulness.

---

421 (God's faithfulness in sending Jesus Christ) Isa 7:14; John 3:17; Gal 4:4; Gen 3:15, 12:3, 22:18; Num 24:17; 2 Sam 7:12-13; Isa 9:7; Deut 18:15

422 (God's faithfulness at the cross) I Cor 1:18; Eph 1:10, 2:15-16; Col 1:20-22, 2:14; Heb 12:2; 2 Cor 5:18; Rom 5:10; 1 John 2:2

423 (God's faithfulness from the beginning) Gen 3:15; Tit 1:2; 2 Tim 1:9; Rom 16:25; Eph 1:4; Matt 13:35

424 (God's faithfulness) Isa 7:14, 9: 6-7; Acts 4:27-28, 13:23; Luke 2:11; Eph 1:4; Ps 33:4, 111:7-9; 2 Thess 3:3; Gen 32:10

"He who did not spare His own Son, but delivered Him over for us all, how will He not also with Him freely give us all things?" [425]

We can truly be assured God will do what He said He would do. We have the record of Scripture that has proven God remembers, fulfills, and has both the knowledge and power to bring everything He promises to pass.

"God is not a man, that He should lie, nor a son of man, that He should repent; Has He said, and will He not do it? Or has He spoken, and will He not make it good?" [426]

↑↓3

GOD'S FAITHFULNESS PRESERVES THE SAINTS

The faithfulness of God is also evident in preserving His Church over thousands of years. Without God's faithfulness to preserve and sustain His children through the harshest of persecutions, [427] there would be no fellowship of Christians. [428]

The heroes of faith were sustained by the faithfulness of God. Hebrews 11 contains a well-known list of people who performed great acts of faith. Each act of faith by these men and women was

---

425 (Salvation is God's great promise) Rom 8:32

426 (God fulfills promises) Num 23:19; I Kin 8:24; 2 Chron 6:10; Ezra 1:1; Matt 1:22, 26:56; Isa 46:8-11; Jer 24:6, 25:12-13; 29:10, 33:14; Amos 9:15; 2 Sam 7:28; Rom 1:2, 3:21, 4:21, 11:29; Tit 1:2; Luke 1:70

427 (God preserves His people) Matt 20:28; 2 Cor 1:22; Eph 1:7, 13-14, 4:30; Rom 3:24; Rev 7:3; Gen 18:17-33, 20:4; Num 16:22

428 (God is faithful to the Church) 1 Cor 1:9, 10:13; Deut 7:9; 2 Cor 1:18; 1 Thess 5:24; 2 Thess 3:3; 2 Tim 2:13; Heb 10:23; 1 John 1:9; Ps 143:1

not faith in their own abilities, but in the faithfulness of God.

> *"The Lord's lovingkindnesses indeed never cease, for His compassions never fail. They are new every morning; great is Your faithfulness."* [429]

↑↓4

God Is Faithful In Disciplining His Children Fairly

God is also faithful in disciplining His children. So faithful is God as a father to us that if we were not being disciplined by Him, we would have to question whether or not we truly were His children. *"Those whom I love, I reprove and discipline; therefore be zealous and repent."*[430]

This is actually a promise and demonstration of God's faithfulness in our sanctification. It is part of the process God uses to bring us closer to Him and conform us to the image of Christ. If God did not do this, we would have to assume we were under judgment, which is punitive, rather than discipline, which is corrective.

↑↓5

He Is Also Faithful To Carry Out Justice

Perhaps there is no difficulty in believing God is faithful in keeping His promises of blessing. We are often eager to accept good things from God's hand, but then we do not believe

---

429 (God's faithfulness is great) Lam 3:22-23; Ps 36:5, 89:8, 119:90; Deut 7:9; Neh 1:5, 9:32; 2 Tim 2:13; Dan 9:4

430 (God is faithful to discipline His children) Rev 3:19; Job 5:17; Ps 94:12; Prov 3:11, 12:1, 23:12; I Cor 11:32; Heb 12:5-11

God means what He says when it comes to the terrifying things such as judgment. God's faithfulness applies not only to blessings, but also to all of the judgments described in Scripture.

Just as everyone outside of Noah's ark was subjected to God's wrath and punishment, so everyone outside of Christ will be subjected to God's coming wrath and judgment. When Christ returns, Scripture is careful to point out He is called *"Faithful and True"* and *"He judges and wages war."* [431] Christ's return for judgment is also a demonstration of God's faithfulness.

At the great white throne judgment, all of humanity will witness the faithfulness of God. [432] The entire course of human history will be examined, and no sin outside of Christ's atonement will remain unpunished, nor will any deed done for God's glory go unrewarded.

Every thought, word, and deed will be brought to account. [433] The books will be opened, and there will be both terror and exhilaration as God's faithfulness to His word comes to pass before everyone's eyes.

We can know God is faithful, and we can see God's faithfulness in action in the Scriptures and history. We have every reason to trust in God's faithfulness, no matter who we are or what we have been through in life. *"The Lord's hand is not so short that it cannot save."* [434]

---

431 (Jesus is Faithful and True in judgment) Rev 19:11

432 (Everyone will witness the faithfulness of God) Rev 20:11-15

433 (God is faithful in judgment) Eccl 3:17; Jer 26:3; Matt 16:27, 25:46; Rev 20:13; 2 Cor 5:10; Rom 1:18-20, 2:6-11, 14:12; 2 Thess 1:6-10; Heb 9:27, 12:27-29; Deut 32:39-42; Ps 1:5-6, 5:5, 7:11, 76:7, 95:10-11; Job 8:3; Num 14:23

434 (God is faithful to save) Isa 59:1; Isa 50:2; Num 11:23; 1 Thess 5:23; 2 Thess 3:3; Zech 3:17; John 17:11, 15; Jude 1:1; Rom 8:32

God is faithful to all who are His; no one will be disappointed who trusts in the Lord. The universe can be undone far more easily than God not making good on His promises in His Word.

"Your lovingkindness, O Lord, extends to the heavens, Your faithfulness reaches to the skies." [435]

↑↓6

SUMMARY

In this chapter, we meditated on trusting in the great faithfulness of God. Everything about God is faithful, and in contrast to sinful human beings, He will never betray us or forsake us. His faithfulness flows out of His truthfulness, and one of the names of God in Scripture is actually "Faithful and True."

We read in the Scriptures about all the promises God has faithfully kept across the ages, not the least of which was the promise of the Messiah in Isaiah and elsewhere as fulfilled by the birth of Christ. He has been faithful to preserve believers through centuries of persecution and to discipline them faithfully as His children. He also faithfully carries out justice on evildoers. God is faithful to all who belong to Him, and not one person will be disappointed who trusts in the Lord. We are humbled by this truth and we should rejoice and *trust* in His faithful nature. As the old hymn so accurately says, "Great is Thy faithfulness, O God my Father."

---

435 (God's faithfulness is incomprehensible) Ps 36:5, NASB

Contemplations

↑↓1

Lord, bring to my mind areas in which I've been unfaithful to You. How have I been unfaithful before You redeemed me? How have I been unfaithful all this time that I've been Your child? How have I been unfaithful this past week? Bring these to mind as I write them down and seek Your forgiveness and restoration in Christ.

↑↓2

Do I understand the altogether different-ness of who You are? Do I understand this even in part? As I meditate on Your faithfulness, Your truthfulness, and Your omniscience, reveal to me fresh insights into who You are. Teach me how to mingle all three facets together as I worship and adore You and help me to worship You in a greater, more expanded way.

↑↓3

How many promises have You made in Your Word? Lead me in my study to know how I might count them. At the same time, I already know they are numerous. What should I glean from counting them? Or what could I glean by simply recognizing the myriad of promises You've made and kept—and promises You have yet to fulfill perfectly.

↑↓4

As I re-read Hebrews 11, teach me how I have made this chapter about the people in that chapter rather than how I should be thinking of You and Your faithfulness. Why have I so often read the Bible thinking about myself and others rather than thinking about You? Help me, by Your grace, to see You in Your beauty in the pages of the Bible.

↑↓5

How much more deeply do You want me to understand Your love in disciplining me and others who are Your children? I certainly understand the concept of loving discipline, but I fear I've not plumbed the depths sufficiently to worship You more fully in this area. My sanctification . . . holiness . . . Your glory . . . Your discipline and correction of me . . . on and on. How may I see more of You in these areas and also more of the glory of Your plan in my life and my life to come after death?

↑↓6

How would You strengthen my faith in You, Lord? If I were to die today, am I confident that I am Yours? Let me ponder my position in Jesus Christ and whether I am actually saved. If I am saved, I know I am secure and in Your hand, but let me pray and ponder my relationship with You, my eternal security in You.

Chapter 17

GOD IS GOOD

"You are good and do good."

Psalm 119:68

THE TRUE DEFINITION AND DEPTH OF GOD'S GOODNESS

People have many uses for the word "good." We may say things or circumstances are good or the weather is good. We may call certain people good when we think highly of them. But when we use the word "good" to describe God's nature, it goes beyond our regular and casual usage. The goodness of God has to be defined with the power and depth shown in the Scriptures.

In fact, our understanding of all things "good" should be rooted in who God is because He alone is the source of all goodness. [436]

---

436 (All goodness is from God) James 1:17; Mark 10:18; Matt 19:17; Ps 25:8, 85:12, 100:5, 106:1, 119:68, 145:9; Nah 1:7

As we seek to understand goodness, a wariness is warranted. We often mistakenly determine goodness by our own parameters, our preferences, or what is to our benefit, rather than the measure of God's goodness as we find it in Scripture. Instead, good should be understood as those things in which God approves and delights. [437] Even the English word "God" has its origins in "the good."

The goodness of God is an essential attribute of God's nature. Scripture tells us, *"God is Light, and in Him there is no darkness at all."* [438] God's goodness does not come from anything other than Himself, and is not based on God doing good things. [439] Instead, when God does good things, it comes from God's goodness.

We know that God never changes [440] and, therefore, we can understand that God's goodness will never increase or decrease. We couldn't desire God to be any more "good" than He already is because He is *infinitely* good. [441] We should not think of God as being anything other than good, regardless of what our personal circumstances may be. [442]

We may find ourselves in unpleasant or painful circumstances in which we question the goodness of God. However, it is important that we understand God is good apart from our personal percep-

---

437 (God delights in goodness) Matt 3:17, 17:5, 25:23; Jer 9:24; 2 Pet 1:17; Isa 42:1; Col 1:10; 1 Thess 4:1; Eph 5:10
438 (God is completely good) 1 John 1:5; James 1:17; Ps 25:8, 86:5, 100:5, 106:1, 119:68; Jer 33:11; Gen 1:4
439 (God is intrinsically good) Ps 25:8; Ps 34:8, 100:5, 106:1, 107:1; 1 Chr 16:34; 2 Chr 5:13
440 (God never changes) Ps 102:25-27; Mal 3:6; James 1:17; Heb 6:18, 13:8; Isa 41:4; Num 23:19; Rom 11:29; Tit 1:2; Lam 3:22
441 (God is always good) Neh 9:20; Ps 25:8, 86:5, 100:5, 106:1, 119:68; 1 Chr 16:34; 2 Chr 5:13; Ezra 3:11; Jer 33:11; Nah 1:7
442 (Our circumstances do not change God's goodness) 1 Thess 5:18; Job 1:20-22; Eph 5:20; 1 Tim 6:7; Col 3:17; 2 Thess 1:3

tion of what is good, and beyond our own circumstances, no matter how difficult they may be.

Especially in hard times, it is easy to think we know what would be good for us, but the Bible is clear that we often desire things that are not good. [443] In fact, we may even find ourselves equating that which is *personally profitable or desirable* with good. But this isn't what the Bible defines as good. [444]

EVIDENCE OF HIS GOODNESS CAN BE SEEN EVERYWHERE

God's goodness can be seen in everything, from His commands, His creation, His laws, and His providence. [445] God's goodness can be seen in all of creation. In the beginning, God made everything and saw that *"it was very good."* [446]

God's goodness extends to all creatures, as He supplies their every need.

> *"The eyes of all look to You, and You give them their food in due time. You open Your hand and satisfy the desire of every living thing."* [447]

God's goodness extends to people. Even the way our bodies are designed tells us about the goodness of God who made them. We

443 (By nature, we desire things that aren't good) Gen 6:5, 8:21; Rom 1:21, 8:7-8; Eph 4:17-19; Mark 7:21-23; Ps 58:3; Matt 15:19; James 4:4; 2 Pet 2:18
444 (Biblical examples of good) Ps 25:8; Ps 34:8, 86:5, 106:1; Mark 10:18; 1 Tim 2:3, 4:4; Heb 6:5
445 (All that God does is good) 1 Tim 4:4; Gen 1:31; Gen 50:20; 1 Tim 1:8; Rom 7:12; Rom 8:28; Ps 19:7; Eccl 3:14
446 (All God made was good) Gen 1:4, 10, 12, 18, 21, 25, 31; Eccl 7:29; 1 Tim 4:4
447 (God's providence is good) Ps 145:15-16; Ps 25:7-8, 104:28, 145:9, 147:8; Acts 10:38; Rom 2:4, 8:28; Gen 45:5, 7, 50:20

have hands that are crafted to do the work given to us. Even the eyes enabling you to read the text on this page are a testimony of the goodness of God! We have plenty of reason to say with the Psalmist, *"I will give thanks to You, for I am fearfully and wonderfully made; wonderful are Your works, and my soul knows it very well."* [448]

We can also see God's goodness in all of creation as He provides variety in the beauty of nature. Next time you go for a walk, consider all of the various things of beauty that are not essential to existence. What does it matter that one flower smells different from another? Why do birds have beautiful designs with an assortment of colors, and why does each species sing unique songs? These are all part of the world God has created with such diversity.

God has provided pleasures for His creatures. That we can experience pleasure is a gift from God. God could have just made food for the stomach without the pleasures or varieties of foods. But He didn't; God wants us to enjoy life—as He designed it. We can gaze upon the beauty of creation and be moved to praise the Lord who made all of it!

God's goodness is so abundant that it becomes easy in our sinfulness to forget about it and take it for granted. [449] Then when trouble comes, we become disgruntled. Then we question the goodness of God, wondering, "If God is so good, then why is He allowing these troubles in my life?" Our pondering does not diminish God's goodness but instead serves to heighten it! [450]

---

448 (God's works are good) Ps 139:14; Ps 40:5, 72:18, 77:14, 86:10, 136:4; Ex 15:11; Job 9:10, 37:5
449 (God's goodness is easily presumed on) Deut 4:9, 23, 32:18; Isa 51:12-13, 65:11-12; Ps 78:11, 106:7, 13, 19-22; Heb 13:16; Prov 1:24; Jer 7:13
450 (God's greatness) Jer 10:6; Ps 18:3, 86:8, 10, 96:4, 136:4; 1 Chr 29:11; Neh 1:5; Ex 15:11

God's Goodness Is Reflected In His Mercy Toward Us

Though it can be hard for us to see, the goodness of God can be completely consistent with our difficulties. If God's goodness meant that everything bad was immediately swept away, then who could stand? We ourselves would be destroyed! No one is innocent, we all sin, yet we're afforded each next breath by God's goodness and mercy! [451] God's goodness is seen in all of the ways He affords wicked people to continue to live. While there is great sorrow and suffering, there is far more blessing in the world. [452]

↑↓1

Consider the very first instance in which people disobeyed God. God could have decided to withhold any blessing from Adam and Eve. However, God gave us a beautiful picture of His goodness. Instead of only pronouncing judgment and walking away, God promised the Messiah and gave animal skins to Adam and Eve to replace their own clothing made of fig leaves. [453] That God would do anything for Adam and Eve after such disobedience is cause to rejoice and celebrate God's goodness as "mercy triumphs over judgment!" [454]

And in the following generations, God has continued to provide mercy for sinners. [455] While we are all guilty and deserving of wrath, God has done something for sinners that is com-

---

451 (God is good to sinners) Ps 4:1, 123:3; Eph 2:4, 7; Ps 86:5, 100:5, 145:9; Heb 4:16; Jer 23:6; Isa 54:17
452 (God's goodness is everywhere) Gen 1:31; Ps 31:19-20, 34:8, 86:5, 100:5, 145:9; Rom 7:12; 1 Tim 4:4
453 (God gave Adam and Eve better clothing) Gen 3:7, 21
454 (Mercy triumphs over judgment) James 2:13
455 (God is good to all) Matt 5:45; Luke 6:35; Acts 14:17; Eph 5:1; Phil 2:15; Num 10:32; Deut 28:12; Ps 65:10, 145:9, 147:8

pletely undeserved and marvelous. God sent Jesus Christ, the perfect Son of God, whom the Father treasures, to people who do not deserve Him. The response of mankind to such goodness was to betray, reject, and generally despise Him.

The cross most wonderfully and incomprehensibly demonstrates the goodness of God. Here, Jesus Christ showed us the highest love possible when He laid down His life for sinners. [456] God's goodness wasn't coerced or grudgingly demonstrated; it was given to us according to His good pleasure, as Scripture tells us:

> *"But the Lord was pleased to crush Him, putting Him to grief;*
> *If He would render Himself as a guilt offering, He will see His*
> *offspring, He will prolong His days, and the good pleasure of*
> *the LORD will prosper in His hand."* [457]

↑↓2

God's goodness is truly a marvelous and wonderful truth. Carefully consider the response people make to this goodness since it is where man's responsibility is most heavily weighted. All people, everywhere, are accountable for their response to the wonderful goodness of God.

GOD'S GOODNESS DOES NOT MEAN HE OVERLOOKS SIN

We must exercise great care when we juxtapose the benevolent goodness of God and His righteous judgment on sin. As with all of His other attributes, we cannot pit one against an-

456 (Jesus died for sinners) John 10:11, 17, 15:13; Rom 4:26, 5:6-8; Eph 5:2; 1 John 3:16, 4:9-10; Matt 20:28; Mark 10:45
457 (The Father sending the Son to suffer is God's goodness) Isa 53:10, NASB; Isa 53:4; John 3:17, 5:36, 38, 6:29, 57, 7:29, 17:18, 20:21

other. We should not think that God's goodness overrides or cancels out His justice. It is because God is good that He serves justice! [458] The very thing many people are mistakenly trusting in will turn out to be the very thing that condemns them.

And yet some believe God's goodness means He is willing to overlook our sinful response. The foolishness of this belief is shown when we see the seriousness of God's response to sin, that He was willing to sacrifice His own Son! [459] God is not willing to overlook any sin, regardless of how desperately we may want Him to. Instead, sin was dealt with on the cross, or paid for in eternity, with more anguish than we can imagine. [460] How great it is to taste the mercies and lovingkindness of God! The goodness of God should move us to repentance and obedience. The promises and commands of God are heard by His sheep, and they follow Him wherever He goes. The goodness of God also means they can trust Him and they know these Scriptural truths in their hearts:

> *"Surely goodness and mercy shall follow me all the days of my life, and I shall dwell in the house of the LORD forever."* [461]

> *"And we know that for those who love God all things work together for good, for those who are called according to His purpose."* [462]

---

458 (God's judgment) Matt 16:27, 25:31-34, 41; Acts 10:42, 17:31, 24:25; John 5:22; 1 Pet 1:17; Rev 19:1-2; 2 Cor 5:10

459 (God is serious about sin) John 6:37-40; Isa 53:5-6, 10; 1 John 4:9-10; Eph 5:2; Rom 4:25, 5:6, 8, 32; Matt 20:28

460 (Sin must be dealt with) Matt 3:12; Matt 13:40-42, 24:51; John 15:6; Rev 14:10-11, 18:18, 19:3, 20:10; Isa 34:10; Gen 19:28

461 (God's children know God's goodness) Ps 16:11, 21:6, 23:5-6, 27:4, 36:8, 45:7, 65:4; Acts 10:38; Isa 25:6; Jer 31:12-14

462 (God is good to His children) Rom 8:28; Rom 5:2, 9:24; 2 Tim 1:9; Jer 31:12-14; Zeph 3:17; Ps 37:4, 147:11; Matt 7:11

↑↓3

Summary

God's goodness is a marvelous and wonderful truth. But we often mistakenly determine goodness by our own parameters rather than looking to Scripture to understand His goodness. No matter how painful our life situation may be, we should still keep in mind, always, that God is good and has only our best interests in mind. We saw how the evidence of God's goodness is seen everywhere in Creation, especially in the fact that He created pleasures all around us. From music and colors to birdsong and the scent of flowers, the abundance of beauty in nature is evidence of His goodness. And lastly, we rejoice at how the cross most wonderfully demonstrates the goodness of God.

Contemplations

↑↓1

Father, it is only the discovery of Your goodness that can banish my fears, lure me into Your presence, and help me to be overwhelmed with grief for my sins and confess them. Help me discover Your goodness so I can live in that beautiful place.

↑↓2

Great was Your goodness, Lord, in undertaking my redemption, in consenting to be made sin for me, and in conquering all my foes.

Today, let me fall to my knees in gratitude for that goodness. There is no one like You in all of heaven and earth!

↑↓3

Lord God of all kindness and light, when You are absent, all sorrows are here, and when You are present, all blessings are mine. Help me, Father, through a mindset of constant prayer, to live in Your presence and remember Your goodness each and every day.

Chapter 18

ABIDING LOVE

"Beloved, let us love one another, for love is from God, and whoever loves has been born of God and knows God. Anyone who does not love does not know God, because God is love. In this the love of God was made manifest among us, that God sent His only Son into the world, so that we might live through Him."

1 John 4:7-9

GOD LOVES BECAUSE IT IS IN HIS NATURE

Although love is affirmed as an essential ingredient in relationships, there seems to be a struggle in contemporary culture to define exactly what it is. If we were to survey various groups of people in society, we would no doubt receive conflicting answers. Fortunately, Scripture is clear to tell us what love is and distinguish it from all of the contradictions of modern society.

"Love is patient and kind; love does not envy or boast; it is not arrogant or rude. It does not insist on its own way; it is not irri-

215

table or resentful; it does not rejoice at wrongdoing, but rejoices with the truth. Love bears all things, believes all things, hopes all things, endures all things." [463]

However, love is more than an action or a single attribute of God. Scripture actually says *"God is love."* [464] God loves because it is His nature; it is who He is. Because the Bible is a record of God's dealings with mankind, we can be sure to find abundant demonstrations of His love.

"All the paths of the LORD are steadfast love and faithfulness, for those who keep His covenant and His testimonies." [465]

THE LORD'S LOVE IS ETERNAL AND UNCHANGING

The love of God is infinite. [466] God's love has immeasurable depth and is as limitless as God's own being. [467] Nothing can restrain His love. [468] God's love surpasses the magnitude and complexity of the finite universe. If the universe is too great for our minds to comprehend fully, then so much more is His infinite love toward His children! The Bible says the love that God has for us is a *"great love with which He loved us."* [469]

---

463 (Definition of love) 1 Cor 13:4-7; Col 3:14; 1 John 3:1, 4:8, 10, 16; Matt 5:44-45; John 3:16; Rom 5:8

464 (God is love) 1 John 3:1, 4:8, 16, 12-13; Ps 86:15; Eph 2:4

465 (God loves us) Ps 25:10; 1 John 3:16; 2 Cor 13:11; Isa 43:4

466 (God's love is infinite) Jer 31:3; Ps 103:8, 136:1-26; Isa 45:17, 54:8-9; Eph 1:3-5, 2:4-5; Hos 11:4; Deut 33:3, 7:7-9

467 (God's love is as infinite as God's own being) Ps 147:5; Isa 40:28; Jer 31:3, 32:17; Matt 19:26; Rom 11:33-34

468 (Nothing can restrain God's love) Rom 8:35; John 10:28, 16:33; Ps 103:17; 1 Pet 4:12-14; 1 John 5:11

469 (God's love is great) Eph 2:4, 7; Jer 31:3; 1 Tim 1:14; Ps 86:5, 15, 100:5; 103:8-11; John 3:16; Eph 3:19; Deut 7:8

God's love is eternal. God's children have always been loved and known by God from eternity, even before their creation. The Lord does not wait for a certain event to occur and use that as a condition for His love. The love of God is unconditional.

> *"Even as He chose us in Him before the foundation of the world, that we should be holy and blameless before Him. In love He predestined us for adoption as sons through Jesus Christ, according to the purpose of His will."* [470]

If you are a child of God, then you can know that God has loved you from all eternity without end. The Lord does not just love you from a distance but desires to be around you now and forever. The Bible reveals that the Lord enjoys and delights in being with his children. [471]

↑↓1

God's love has no source other than Himself. If God's love were set upon us before we were created, then it follows that there is nothing in us as God's creatures that caused God to love us. The reason for His love is found in God's own sovereign will and purpose alone.

> *"Therefore do not be ashamed of the testimony about our Lord, nor of me his prisoner, but share in suffering for the gospel by the power of God, who saved us and called us to a holy calling, not because of our works but because of His own purpose and grace, which He gave us in Christ Jesus before the ages began."* [472]

---

470 (God's love is unconditional) Eph 1:4-5; 2 Tim 1:9; Rom 3:27, 8:28-30; 1 Cor 13:7; Tit 3:5; 1 Pet 1:3; Gal 1:15

471 (God loves being with His children) Rev 7:15, 21:3; Lev 26:11-12; Ezek 37:27; John 1:14, 14:23; 2 Cor 6:16; Heb 11:16; Zeph 3:17

472 (God's love is in His purpose alone) 2 Tim 1:8-9; Deut 7:7-8, 10:15; Rom 5:8, 9:15-16, 18; 1 John 3:1; Tit 3:4-5; Eph 2:4-5; Jer 31:3

God's love does not change. God's love is exactly what it was before time began, and it will continue forever just as it is now. [473] God's love does not change because God Himself does not change. [474] The unchanging nature of God's love means we can depend on it today and, with certainty, tomorrow. [475]

An example of God's unchanging love is found in Scripture concerning the way God relates to Jacob. Jacob suffered from many of the same things we do, including unbelief and disobedience. However, in one of the most shocking statements in Scripture, God says, *"Jacob I loved."* [476] If God were seeking a reason not to love Jacob, He had plenty to choose from. Instead, we find an amazing testimony of God's unshakable and unfailing love!

> *"For I am sure that neither death nor life, nor angels nor rulers, nor things present nor things to come, nor powers, nor height nor depth, nor anything else in all creation, will be able to separate us from the love of God in Christ Jesus our Lord."* [477]

God's Love Is Also Holy And Includes Discipline

As wonderful as all of these qualities of God's love are, it is important to remember that God's love is holy. [478] God's love is not capri-

---

473 (God's love is unchanging) Ex 34:6; Ps 25:6, 36:7, 86:5, 106:45; 1 John 3:1 (compare Eph 1:11); Lam 3:22-23; Luke 1:50; Mal 3:6
474 (God is unchanging) James 1:17; Isa 40:8; Heb 6:18, 13:8; Mal 3:6; Ps 102:27; Num 23:19
475 (God's love is dependable) Prov 3:5, 4:26, 22:19; 1 Pet 5:7; Isa 12:2, 26:4; John 3:16; Ps 37:3, 23; 2 Thess 3:3; Rom 11:29
476 (God loved Jacob) Rom 9:13
477 (Nothing separates us from God's love) Rom 8:38-39; John 10:28, 17:2; Rom 5:8; 1 John 2:25, 4:19, 5:11
478 (God's love is holy) 1 Pet 1:16; 1 John 1:5; Ps 22:3; Isa 6:3, 57:15; Lev 11:44,

cious or rooted in emotional sentiments or some form of weakness. Instead, we should be mindful that the Lord shows His love in holiness and purity. This is a sobering thought, and it should not escape our attention that the Lord's love for His children includes discipline, and it demands righteousness.

"For the Lord disciplines the one He loves, and chastises every son whom He receives." [479]

God is under no obligation to show love, but He demonstrates it as He chooses. In Romans 9:13, while we read that God loved Jacob, He also hated Esau. These were twin children born to the same parents at the same time, so there was no reason to love one over the other. This is a solemn reminder that God's love isn't forced or coerced by anyone. Instead, Scripture teaches clearly that God's love is according to His own purpose and will.

"In love He predestined us to adoption as sons through Jesus Christ to Himself, according to the kind intention of His will." [480]

↑↓2

God's love is gracious. God loves His children because He wants to. It was love and the goodness of God that was expressed when He sent Jesus Christ into the world to pay for sin. The Lord wasn't required to do anything about our disobedience except punish sin. But it pleased the Lord, willingly and graciously, to rescue His chil-

---

19:2, 20:7; Rev 4:8; Luke 1:49

479(God disciplines those He loves) Heb 12:6-8; Rev 3:19; Prov 3:12, 13:24, 23:13; Ps 94:12, 119:67, 75; Deut 8:5; 2 Sam 7:14

480 (God's love is according to His own purpose and will) Eph 1:4-5, 9; Deut 7:7-8; Rom 5:8, 9:15-16, 18; 1 John 3:1; John 14:31; Heb 2:4; Luke 12:32

dren from eternal judgment. The single greatest event in the history of mankind is characterized by love: the cross.

> *"Greater love has no one than this, that someone lay down his life for his friends."* [481]

God has not merely told us that He loves us, but He has demonstrated it by giving us His Son Jesus Christ. The Father gave up His Son, whom He loved, willingly and according to His pleasure, for those who would be adopted into His family.

> *"By this we know love, that He laid down his life for us, and we ought to lay down our lives for the brothers."* [482]

WE ARE CALLED TO LOVE GOD BACK AND TO LOVE OTHERS AS HE DOES

God also commands us to *"love the Lord your God with all your heart and with all your soul and with all your mind."* Christians are called to love the Lord, not just be recipients of His love. God's love for us causes us to respond with love and say, *"We love because He first loved us."* [483]

God's love also calls Christians to love others. Jesus has said that we are to love our neighbor and to love our enemies, even those who mock and persecute us. [484] Scripture tells us that one of the ways we demonstrate that we belong to the Lord is by our love for one another.

---

481 (The cross is God's greatest love) John 15:13; Eph 2:4, 5:2; 1 John 3:16, 4:7-11; John 3:16, 10:11; Tit 3:4-5; Rom 5:7-8, 8:37; 2 Thess 2:16

482 (We love the brethren with this same love) 1 John 3:16, 4:9-11, 20-21; John 13:34; Phil 2:17; Lev 19:18; Rom 13:8; Col 3:14; 1 Thess 4:9; 1 Tim 1:5; 1 Pet 1:22

483 (We love because He loved first) 1 John 2:10, 4:10, 4:19; Luke 7:47; Gal 5:22; 2 Cor 5:14-15; John 15:16; 2 Tim 2:22

484 (Love even those who mock and persecute us) Matt 5:44; Rom 12:14, 20; 1 Pet 3:9; Prov 25:21-22; Luke 6:27-28, 34-35; Ex 23:4

"By this all men will know that you are My disciples, if you have love for one another." [485]

Love has an amazing power to join people together. It joined the Church to Jesus Christ, and it joins the members of the Church to each other. If we're going to be known by our love, then we need to know Him who is love. The more we understand God's own amazing love, the more we will be drawn to Him! Jesus prayed concerning the unity of Christians; therefore, let us endeavor to love one another!

"I do not ask for these only, but also for those who will believe in me through their word, that they may all be one, just as You, Father, are in me, and I in You, that they also may be in Us, so that the world may believe that You have sent Me. The glory that You have given Me I have given to them, that they may be one even as We are one, I in them and You in me, that they may become perfectly one, so that the world may know that You sent me and loved them even as You loved me. Father, I desire that they also, whom You have given Me, may be with Me where I am, to see My glory that You have given Me because You loved Me before the foundation of the world." [486]

↑↓3

Summary

In this chapter, we meditated on God's deep and unending love

485 (Disciples are known for their love for each other) John 13:35, 17:21; 1 John 2:4, 9, 3:10-14, 4:12, 20-21
486 (Jesus' prayer that we know the Father loved us) John 17:20-24

and how by His very nature He is love. His love is also eternal. His children have always been loved and known by God from eternity, even before creation. But His love also includes discipline, and the Scriptures make it clear that God disciplines His children, the ones He loves. It is, of course, only for our good and to bring us into right relationship with Him and with others. Sending Jesus to die in our place on the cross was God's highest act of love for us. As believers, we are called to love Him back, and to love others in the same way He loves them.

CONTEMPLATIONS

↑↓1

Lord, You are love. Like so many of your attributes, You are the *embodiment* of love. I can only understand love by virtue of my understanding of who You are. Love is not who I am, but love is who You are. No other god claims love for its people the way You do. You are unlike all other gods—You are the one true God and Your love is the seal on that truth.

Your love is eternal because You entered into a covenant with me. You keep your promises . . . that I know full well. And because You do not fail to keep Your promises, I can know that Your love will never fail or end. You would never break a covenant that You made. Your word endures forever, as does Your love. So help me to stop trying to earn Your love. Let my obedience be an outpouring of my heart of love for You, not for some effort to tip the scales in my favor.

Perhaps the greatest gulf between Your love and mine is the conditions I place on my love before offering it. My mind cannot absorb how You can continue to love me in spite of the seemingly endless ways I have offended You. My love changes all the time, while yours never changes. I have no other choice but to worship when I consider all that Your love endures.

↑↓2

Lord, from You, through You, and to You are all things—*especially* Your love. There is nothing in me that warrants Your love. Why did You choose me, Lord? There have been trillions of people throughout human history—why do You love me? I don't know, but as the song goes, I'm so glad You did! I could have been Esau, but You adopted me into the same family as Jacob. I cannot fathom Your gracious choice, but help me to receive it with grace and let my response be a great affection for You that drives out sin.
Your love is Holy. This is in stark contrast to man's love, which is rooted in sin. It means that Your love is unquestionably without fault. 1 Corinthians 13 reminds me of all the ways in which our love fails. But Your love never fails because You never fail. You are perfect in all Your ways; therefore, Your love is perfect. Forgive me for the times I have questioned Your love based on my circumstances. Forgive me for presuming that Your love is like mine, dependent upon actions and events and people.

↑↓3

Lord, help me to remember that the ultimate expression of Your love was the cross. I tend to forget that when I demand of You, when I cite Your love for me as the basis for wanting You to give me what I desire . . . like a petulant child. You have given me the only thing that matters—love that best manifested itself in the most costly of sacrifices. That sacrifice has given me eternity with You, rescuing me from the condemnation that I deserve. What love!

You call me to love you with all my heart, soul, mind, and strength. You command me to love my neighbor as myself. When I meditate on Your love, all I can think about is that You cannot even call my love a cheap replica of Yours. Your love is altogether "other." I can't approximate it. I need Your love to reside in me. I need Your strength to love as I should. A . W . Tozer said, "It takes God to love God." I claim that as my prayer today. Without Your love pouring out of me, what the world gets from me will not be what You want. How weak I am and how strong You are that I need Your help in order to follow Your own commands. Help me to love as I ought—take away my desire for self-advancement; let me diminish so that You might increase, to Your eternal glory.

Chapter 19

THE INCOMPREHENSIBILITY OF GOD

"Oh, the depth of the riches and wisdom and knowledge of God! How unsearchable are His judgments and how inscrutable His ways!"

Romans 11:33

As we reflect back on our adoration of our great and glorious God, the journey has been brief and incomplete. We have likely even made some errors. (Father, please forgive us.) But we have studied enough to be able to form a stronger impression of our Lord. All of us can—and should—learn more about God, yet we also realize that He is beyond us. We can never understand everything about Him. He is incomprehensible. The longer we consider and meditate on His infinite greatness, the more likely we are to utter the words of Zophar from the book of Job:

"Can you find out the deep things of God? Can you find out the limit of the Almighty? It is higher than heaven—what can you

do? Deeper than Sheol—what can you know? Its measure is longer than the earth and broader than the sea." [487]

When we turn our thoughts to God's eternity, His immateriality, His omnipresence, His almightiness, our finite minds are overwhelmed. But just because we can never fully comprehend the divine nature does not mean that we should not humbly ask questions and prayerfully seek and study to grasp what He has so graciously revealed of Himself in His Word. [488] In the end, nothing that we know will we know fully or perfectly, but even though all of our knowledge is imperfect, it would be foolish to say we should not make any efforts to learn anything else. C.H. Spurgeon explains this concept as follows:

> Nothing will so enlarge the intellect, nothing so magnify the whole soul of man, as a devout, earnest, continued, investigation of the great subject of the Deity. The most excellent study for expanding the soul is the science of Christ and Him crucified and the knowledge of the Godhead in the glorious Trinity.
>
> The proper study of the Christian is the Godhead. The highest science, the loftiest speculation, the mightiest philosophy, which can engage the attention of a child of God, is the name, the nature, the person, the doings, and the existence of the great God which he calls his Father. There is something exceedingly improving to the mind in a contemplation of the Divinity.

---

487 (God is incomprehensible) Job 11:7-9; Ps 139:6, 17-18, 147:5; Isa 40:28; Job 5:9; Eccl 3:11, 8:17; Rom 11:33; Eph 3:10

488 (Scripture reveals God) 1 Cor 2:10; Deut 29:29; Eph 3:3, 5; John 14:26, 16:13; 1 John 2:27; Matt 16:17; Gal 1:12, 16

It is a subject so vast, that all our thoughts are lost in its immensity; so deep, that our pride is drowned in its infinity. Other subjects we can comprehend and grapple with; in them we feel a kind of self-content, and go on our way with the thought, "Behold I am wise."

But when we come to this master science, finding that our plumb-line cannot sound its depth, and that our eagle eye cannot see its height, we turn away with the thought "I am but of yesterday and know nothing." [489]

That God is by nature incomprehensible should teach us to proceed with humility, caution, and reverence. [490] After all our studies and examinations and meditations, we have to say with Job, *"Behold, these are but the outskirts of His ways, and how small a whisper do we hear of Him!"* [491]

To paraphrase a quote from Puritan John Howe,

> The Lord has, in His word, given us a true report of Himself, but not a full report. We know enough to keep us from gross error in our further studies, but not enough to keep us from ignorance. We can contemplate the various perfect attributes in which the blessed God reveals His being to us, and can in our thoughts identify them all with Him, even though our grasp of these attributes is still only partial and defective. [492]

---

489 Spurgeon, Charles Haddon. "The Immutability of God." New Park Street Chapel, Southwark. 7 Jan. 1855. Sermon.
490 (Humility before God) 1 Pet 3:8; 1 Pet 5:5-6; James 4:6, 10; Matt 23:12; Prov 29:23; Isa 2:11, 57:15; Luke 1:52; Mic 6:8
491 (God's ways are infinite) Job 26:14; Job 5:9, 9:10; Ps 71:15, 145:3, 147:5; Eccl 3:11; Eph 3:8; 2 Chr 2:6; 1 Tim 6:16
492 Pink, A.W. *Attributes of God.* n.p, 1930. Print.

↑↓1

A tremendous difference exists between the knowledge of God that His people have in this life and what they will have in heaven, but God's incomprehensibility will still remain. Scripture says that as Christians, we shall see Him *"face to face"* and *"know"* even as we are known, [493] but we cannot take this to mean that we will know God as comprehensively as He knows us. He will still be God and we will not. [494] Our knowledge will be accurate and true, but not exhaustive. Glorified Christians will still be finite creatures—never fully able to comprehend their infinite Creator. As A.W. Pink explains,

> They will see Him more clearly, though, than they could ever see Him by corrupt reason and imperfect faith, and more extensively than creation and all of His miracles and Providential works in human history had yet revealed of Him.
>
> Their minds will not be so expanded, though, that they will be capable of grasping all at once, or in extensive detail, His entire excellent nature. To comprehend infinite perfection, they must become infinite themselves. Even in heaven, their knowledge will be partial, but at the same time their happiness will be complete, because their knowledge will be perfect in the sense that it will be sufficient for the scope of the subject, even though it will not know its object exhaustively.

How exciting for Christians to think that once dead and gone to heaven, their knowledge and understanding of God will increase, and as their vision expands, their blessedness will increase. And

---

493 (We will know God truly, but not exhaustively) 1 Cor 13:12; 1 Cor 2:10-12; Ps 139:6, 17, 145:3, 147:5; Rom 11:33; Isa 55:9
494 (Man is not God) 1 Cor 8:6; Num 23:19; Deut 4:35, 39, 6:4; Isa 46:9; Jer 10:6-7; 1 Cor 8:4; 1 Tim 2:5

their understanding of God will never grow past the point where there is nothing more to be discovered, adored and worshipped. Even after ten thousand years in His presence, He will still be the incomprehensible God. [495]

↑↓2

The study of an incomprehensible God also has benefit for us while we live here because it teaches us about ourselves. [496] John Calvin explains,

> Our wisdom, in so far as it ought to be deemed true and solid Wisdom, consists almost entirely of two parts: the knowledge of God and of ourselves . . . . No man can survey himself without also turning his thoughts toward the God in whom he lives and moves. The endowments which we possess cannot possibly be from ourselves; our very being is nothing else than subsistence in God alone.

> . . . Man never attains to a true self-knowledge until he has previously contemplated the face of God . . . . In our pride, we always seem to ourselves to be just, upright, wise and holy, until we are convinced, by clear evidence, of our injustice, vileness, folly, and impurity. [497]

↑↓3

Our contemporary mindset may deem something incomprehen-

---

495 Pink, A.W. *Attributes of God.* n.p, 1930. Print.
496 (We will never exhaust the knowledge of God) Col 1:10; Ps 139:6, 17-18, 147:5; 1 Cor 2:10-12, 13:12; Rom 11:33; Isa 55:9; Eph 3:8
497 Calvin, John. *Institutes of Christian Religion.* Geneva: n.p., 1536. Print.

sible and walk away. What is the point, after all, in trying to understand something that cannot be understood? But too often we want to learn something in great detail so we can become experts. We even say we want to "master" our subject. But mastery is about control, and God will not be controlled. [498] And there is tremendous value in studying Him, contemplating Him, meditating on Him, even if our true knowledge of Him as He is only grows in the slightest amount. [499]

↑↓4

God is worthy of our worship, whether we appreciate Him or not. [500] We should devote our time, our energy, our lives to studying Him, contemplating His character and His ways to learn all that we can. The Lord God is incomprehensible, yes. But He also calls us to pursue Him, to learn from Him, to seek Him while He may be found, [501] to taste and see that He is good (Psalm 34:8).

Now, to the King of the ages, immortal, invisible, the only God, be honor and glory forever and ever. Amen.

1 Timothy 1:17

---

498 (God's purpose cannot be stopped) Job 42:2; Gen 18:14; Isa 14:27, 43:13; Dan 4:31, 35; Eccl 3:14; Prov 19:21; Matt 19:26; Ps 33:10-11

499 (Tremendous value in studying God) Matt 4:4; Deut 8:3; 2 Tim 3:15, 17; Philip 4:19; Hos 4:6; Rom 2:4; 11:33; Isa 5:13; Eph 3:8

500 (God is worthy to be praised) Ps 96:4, 145:3, 147:5, 150:6; Rom 11:33; Dan 4:34-35; 2 Sam 22:4; Rev 4:11, 5:12; 1 Cor 6:19-20

501 (God invites us to know more about Him) Isa 55:3, 6; Isa 45:19, 22, 40:8; Ps 32:6; Amos 5:6; 2 Cor 6:1-2; Rev 22:17

CONTEMPLATIONS

↑↓1

Father, why do I try to put You into a box? Why do I attempt to make a list of who You are and somehow feel satisfied, accomplished? In some ways, I hope You agree that it is good that I categorize, sort, and list so that I might grasp who You are. In other ways, show me my error. Teach me more about how to go beyond what I can comprehend and increase my enjoyment of You, my worship of You. Let me, by Your grace, worship Your incomprehensibility right now!

↑↓2

Perhaps my intimacy with You and my comfort in calling You "Abba, Daddy," has given me a false understanding. In some ways, perhaps I've thought that when I get to heaven, I will know You fully, that I will know a lot, perhaps everything, fully. How absurd is this idea as I reflect on it now. And how exciting to think that forever in eternity I will learn more and more of You! And perhaps the most massive difference in heaven will be when I can relate without my sinful nature dragging me, clouding me. Ahhh, Father, how I yearn to know You more openly and clearly!

↑↓3

I'm learning a higher view, a more accurate view, of You. And I'm peeking into my own self and I don't like it. This is more uncomfortable than I thought it would be. The juggling of new heights of Your greatness with new depths of my sinfulness are tough. How would You have me juggle this? Teach me where my juggling is good and true. Teach me also where my juggling falls apart, where I may be too hard on myself, too much in despair, lacking confidence, comfort, and hope in You.

↑↓4

Control – Huh! How I try to control so many things! I feel it in my flesh. I crave it. And yet, growing in my knowledge of You is strangely two-sided, double-minded; I'm not really sure how to describe it. On great days, when I am meditating with You in Your Word, journaling, I feel so mentally and emotionally stretched, enlivened, excited at the new insights and new intimacy with You. Yet at other times, I grind slowly through the task. Humble me, Lord, because I am so prideful. Keep me thirsty for You. Please give me Your grace to grow and learn in humility and to reflect You and glorify You!

Summary

THE NEXT STEPS ON YOUR CHRISTIAN JOURNEY

If you are like most people, once you read a book, you feel a sense of accomplishment, a sense of completion. Perhaps the next question in your mind is . . . Now what?

Let me suggest several possibilities for you:

Connect with the Adoring God ministry

Give this book to others

Talk with others about God

Start a small group

Structure your quiet time

Journal your prayers

Strengthen your meditation

Focus on God in your Bible

Ponder your relationship with God

Connect with Adoring God Ministry

Visit our website: www.AdoringGod.org. We would enjoy hearing from you about the impact this book has made on your relationship with Christ. We would also appreciate suggestions on how we can improve our materials further. Also, on any of the suggestions below, let us know if you'd like some help.

Give This Book to Others

This book is about Christian meditation, prayer, and reading God's Word. It is about developing and deepening your relationship with God through Jesus Christ. The purpose of life is to glorify God and enjoy Him forever. Let us all help one another to live life with this purpose in mind.

Talk with Others About God

Begin talking with others about who He is, how He acts, what He is doing in your life, and His response to you as you meditate, pray, and read His Word. You will soon discover richer, deeper, more interesting relationships with others as you engage with them about the most important person in the world—God!

Start a Small Group

Perhaps you've just finished this book with a group. If so, consider continuing the group again, working further on one another's meditations, journaling, Bible reading, or prayers. Or create a new group. If you read this book alone, then reach out to others, give them copies of this book, and ask them if they'd like to join you in a small group to discuss a chapter per week together.

Structure Your Quiet Time

Re-think when you have your quiet time and how long you should be spending with God. Grab your calendar; look at how you can readjust in order to spend more time with Him and make Him a bigger priority.

Journal Your Prayers

Continue to journal prayers to God. Rather than just taking notes like you might in a classroom setting, write your prayers to God, talking with Him, asking Him about Himself, telling Him about your feelings and thoughts. Then go back and read over what you've written. Consider ways God is convicting you to change. Identify new areas of doctrine you'd like to meditate on further.

Strengthen Your Meditation

Work your mind and your heart as you read and ponder God's Word. Consider using an online Bible and do a word search that will enable you to read through all of the verses displayed. Read them slowly. Ponder. See how some connect to what you are seeking to understand. Of course, ask God to guide you and provide you with wisdom. Ask Him to show more of Himself and also how you can change and grow in your relationship with Him.

Focus on God in Your Bible

Have you tended to read the Bible merely as an instruction manual for life rather than as a book about God? Determine to read two to three familiar Bible stories and focus on God, rather than the plot or the people in the story. Ask yourself as you read, "What does this story tell me about who God is?" As you write down the characteristics of God that you find, do an online Bible word search and go deeper into who God is.

Ponder Your Relationship with God

Ask yourself the hard question, "How well do I know you, God?" Sit quietly for a good while and consider what kind of relationship you currently have with Him. Perhaps write your thoughts down on a pad of paper to keep your mind organized. Then ask yourself a second question. "How can I know you better, God?" Write more thoughts down. Then take what you've written and do an online Bible search for some of the words that jump out for you. Ask God to reveal Himself to you in new ways as you read about Him in the Bible.

Now may the God of peace who brought again from the dead our Lord Jesus, the great shepherd of the sheep, by the blood of the eternal covenant, equip you with everything good that you may do His will, working in us that which is pleasing in His sight, through Jesus Christ, to whom be glory forever and ever. Amen.

Hebrews 13:20-21

Soli Deo Gloria,

A Final Note

DEEPENING YOUR RELATIONSHIP WITH GOD

When people ask me about this book and what it's about, I tell them it is about the character and personality of God and how I (and others) can best relate to Him through prayer, meditation, and the Bible.

Prayer, meditation, and reading Scripture, when mixed together, form a powerful compound. Scripture grounds our meditations in truth. Meditation takes us deeper into a scriptural truth. Prayer with meditation inflames the heart to adore God and worship Him. Scripture enhances our prayer time and reminds us of truths as we petition and thank Him.

Keeping prayer, meditation, and the reading of Scripture separated from each other limits their value and can even be detrimental to our lives.

Prayer uninformed by Scripture becomes either a recitation of what we already think and believe or merely a litany of our wants and desires.

And even if our prayers are informed by Scripture, without meditation, we will be hindered from gaining a better understanding of who God is and who we are.

Study of the Word without prayer and meditation becomes merely an academic exercise, filling our heads with knowledge but not engaging our hearts.

And meditation—time spent pondering God—without referencing His Word and without petitioning Him to aid our understanding, can amount to merely talking to ourselves, or worse, believing things that are not true.

Prayer

I suspect that a great many Christians may pray *at* God rather than enter into a two-way conversation *with* God. They use prayer to get things from God. They tell Him the list of things they want from Him and they tell Him what they want Him to do for them. Maybe a few thoughts of thankfulness are sprinkled in, too. Such petitions treat God like nothing more than a celestial vending machine.

Many people who focus their prayers on the *character* of God, however, find that their prayers change. Prayers transform into a real conversation with the Almighty Lord of the universe. People find that their prayer times become moments to know Him better and to enjoy His presence above everything else.

In your prayers, consider telling God you want to know Him for His own sake. Let Him reveal Himself to you in His Word. Ask Him to show Himself to you in new ways. Adore Him. Worship Him simply because of who He is and not just for what you get from Him as a result. Move beyond prayers that merely thank God for what He has done for you, to adoration and praise that is focused on who God is.

As we discover how infinitely big God really is, we can also feel how puny we really are. In your prayers, ask God to reveal things about yourself and your relationship with Him. Tell Him how you really feel and think, and be really honest and open with Him.

Don't ignore promptings in God's Word and from the Holy Spirit that may cause you pain as you recognize your sinfulness and other errors. And be sure to recognize the gospel and what Jesus Christ has done on the cross for those He loves. If you are a Christian, confess any sins that may be exposed, repent and recognize the finished work of Christ having paid the penalty for your sins, and crawl affectionately into Abba Father's lap, resting in the glorious gospel.

Your Prayer Journal

I am a very strong proponent of keeping a prayer journal. I find that my mind is far too prone to wander if I do not do something to anchor it in the activity of meditation. My flesh is weak and the devil prowls about, so I find that journaling is a great tool to organize and protect my meditations.

Also, most of us retain information much better by taking notes while reading a textbook rather than by just passing our eyes across the page. Lastly, if you are using this book in a group study, sharing the thoughts in your journals can form a centerpiece to your time together.

Remember, too, that this is not *just* a journal but a *prayer* journal. Write toward God. This is still prayer; you are not writing a study outline for a college exam. Make it intimate, God-focused, and God-centered. Do not be afraid to write out your emotions and thoughts, even and especially those that may feel messy, wrong, or ugly. The Lord knows our hearts better than we do. It is best to be honest with Him and ourselves. And don't worry about grammar, structure, or spelling. You can journal by jotting down bullet points or a string of unrelated notes rather than perfect sentences. The purpose of journaling is not to produce a fancy written dissertation to be graded by a theology professor. It is used as a tool to grow in your intimacy with the Lord. He is your only audience, unless you choose to share with other believers. If you are uncomfortable, however, with what you wrote, then know that you have permission to throw it away or burn it.

Meditation

I hope this book has helped you move beyond prayer techniques and information-based Bible study and on to true and genuine meditation on the truths you learn. Be still. Quiet yourself. Concentrate. Think deeply on Him, on doctrines, on concepts of life and theology. Do not simply recite beliefs or doctrines without considering their implications or even their contradictions. God's infiniteness deserves more than a passing thought.

Acknowledge that thinking can be hard and may even hurt at times if you're not used to it. For many, the "brain muscles" may need to be exercised and strengthened by God's grace.

If you find meditation difficult, perhaps because it is new, be honest and include that in your journal. Jot down notes of what you are struggling with (my mind is too distracted, I'm not used to carving out time for this, etc.) and address these very issues in your further meditations. Don't surrender to your present frailties, but seek God's help to solve those difficulties. You may engage with Him and arrive at some resolutions on your own or you may want to enlist the help of your pastor or some other believer who cares about you.

By God's grace, an important goal of meditation is to kindle the flame of your affections for God. Meditation should enhance your ability to love Him with all your heart and mind and soul and strength. The more you meditate on His character, His works, and His ways, the more you should passionately adore Him.

Reading Scripture

View Scripture as a way to grow in your relationship with the Lord. Sadly, I think many Christians simply read the Bible for an inspiring word or encouraging promise for the day. These are legitimate reasons, but God has so much more to say to us! Read the Bible to learn about God Himself and Who He is, His likes and dislikes, and His plans and purposes. Don't read the Word merely because you think by doing so you can make life work for you, as if you were reading a manual to a lawnmower or household appliance. Don't read it just to figure out how you can get something more from the Christian life. Pursue God for His own sake.

As you read the historical portions of Scripture, the storyline and the characters are important, but God is the main character on every page. Read the Bible to see how His character is revealed and how our understanding of Him developed.

Time and Effort

Focused prayer, study, and meditation requires time. An hour or more at a time is probably ideal, much better than a mere five or ten minutes of Scripture reading and quickly uttered prayer. You may need to rearrange your schedule and your calendar to make this possible. Many of us already feel pressed for time as it is, but I challenge you to assess what is truly important in your life and what is not.

This is not a prescriptive, legalistic standard, but a practical, logistical reality. It can be difficult to understand and assimilate eternal truths and profound concepts of our glorious God by only spending teeny tiny snippets of time studying Him.

Recognize, too, that there will be numerous obstacles and hindrances to the pursuit of God through prayer, Scripture reading, and meditation. The devil strives through distraction and temptation to keep us from our pursuit of God.

Also, our sinful flesh within us is a willing participant in Satan's schemes, always naturally seeking to ignore Him. If we are honest, we often simply don't want to pray, read Scripture, or meditate. We would rather indulge in our self-centered preoccupations—we constantly need God's grace to fight these tendencies.

Sometimes we have physical infirmities that range from temporary sleepiness to long-term health conditions that make it difficult for us to remain stationary and engaged mentally for long periods of time. Others may have mental or cognitive infirmities that limit their capacities for deep or frequent meditation.

Some may find the process daunting, simply due to unfamiliarity and lack of experience. Many are burdened with the numerous distractions of modern life. For some who may be in a particularly bad season, those distractions can seem overwhelming.

Don't let these or other trials deter you from an eager pursuit of God. Rather, let them motivate you all the more, as He is the only answer to life's hardships. Pray for God to help you so you do not avoid the undertaking altogether. With God's aid, pursue Him!

Perhaps your pursuit of God will not be easy. Most things of great value usually require more effort and cost us. But knowledge of the Almighty and increased, improved fellowship with Him is worth the effort and the discipline when you consider the delight, the joy, the holiness, and the peace that could be yours in Him. May this book be a major catalyst of change in your Christian life, and may God be magnified and receive all the glory!

ABOUT ADORING GOD

Today, many Christians are unfamiliar with the astounding beauty of God.

The ministry of Adoring God is devoted to sharing the truth of who God is and how to enjoy Him deeply. We want to help sharpen your mind, soften your heart, and expand your soul as you seek to know the glory of God.

By God's grace, many people have found a new spring in their steps as they walk with Jesus Christ through our materials and group studies. By focusing more clearly on the true God of the Bible, many facets of your Christian life can be transformed—how you read the Scriptures, listen to a sermon, pray, think, act, and speak.

If you want to go deeper in your relationship with God, then the message and ministry of *Adoring God* is one of your best resources. May you be blessed in your journey.

www.AdoringGod.org

SUPPLEMENTAL READING

Knowing God
   by J.I. Packer

A Passion for God: Prayers and Meditations on the Book of Romans
   by Raymond C. Ortlund, Jr

Abba's Child
   by Brennan Manning

Attributes of God
   by A.W. Pink

The Attributes of God
   by R.C. Sproul

Counterfeit Gods
   by Tim Keller

God's Greater Glory
   by Bruce Ware

Holiness
   by J.C. Ryle

Love the Lord with All Your Mind
   by J.P. Moreland

Meditation
  by Nathaniel Ranew

Pleasures Forevermore
  by Sam Storms

Taste and See
  by John Piper

The Enemy Within
  by Kris Lundgaard

The Existence and Attributes of God
  by Stephen Charnock

The Knowledge of the Holy
  by A.W. Tozer

The Papa Prayer
  by Larry Crabb

The Pleasures of God
  by John Piper

The Pressure's Off
  by Larry Crabb

The Pursuit of God
  by A.W. Tozer

The Pursuit of Holiness
  by Jerry Bridges

The Valley of Vision
  by Arthur Bennett, Editor

When I Don't Desire God
  by John Piper

ABOUT THE AUTHOR

In 2009, Keith Knell started the ministry of Adoring God (www. AdoringGod.org). His vision is to share the truth of who God is and how to enjoy Him more deeply. Over the years, Keith has taught numerous groups how to blend Bible-reading, prayer, and Christian meditation in one's walk with the Lord. By God's grace, many people have found a new spring in their steps as they walk with Jesus Christ through Adoring God's group studies and materials.

In addition to Keith Knell's work with Adoring God, he is President and CEO of One Trusted Advisor (www.OneTrustedAdvisor. com). Keith's education as both an accountant and attorney, and his extensive experience in business and finance, enable him to provide a wide array of tax, financial, business, and legal counsel. He is gifted at making the complex easy to understand and helping clients to see how the whole is greater than the sum of the parts.